A
Charlie Parker
STUDY ALBUM

Edited
with transcriptions and
biographical and analytical notes by
LIONEL GRIGSON

Parts for B♭ and E♭ instruments are inserted

NOVELLO
London and Sevenoaks

Cat. No. 11 0219

Text and compilation © Copyright 1989 Novello & Company Limited
8-10 Lower James Street, London W1R 3PL   Tel: 01-287 5060

ISBN 0 85360 140 2

Cover photograph: William Gottlieb/Redferns
                © Redferns   Used by permission

German translations by Jennifer Casey
French translations by Peter Owens
Translations © 1989 Novello & Company Limited

Novello & Co. Ltd gratefully acknowledges the generous assistance of the Atlantic
Music Corp. in allowing access to the Charlie Parker copyrights for the
preparation of this volume.

The Editor wishes to acknowledge the contribution of Leslie East in conceiving
and developing this project for publication.

Contents   *Inhalt*   *Table des Matières*

Transcriptions (preceded by Piano Versions)

Transkriptionen (denen Versionen für klavier vorausgehen):

Transcriptions (précedées par les versions pour piano)

Übersetzungen der Einführung ins Deutsche und Französische sind zwischen S.20 und S.53 zu finden.

Les traductions françaises et allemandes des notes d'introduction se trouvent entre les pages 20 et 53.

The difference of a 4th in the ranges of alto and tenor saxophones creates difficulties in transferring solos from one instrument to the other. Played as written from the B♭ parts, each solo contains a few notes below the tenor range. However, a tenor saxophonist with a good command of the upper register should be able to play the B♭ parts an octave higher. Either way, though, if played in the original keys the solos are not really suited to the tenor range. A solution is to read the E♭ parts on tenor, thus using Parker's fingering. (In this case the accompaniment must be transposed down a 4th or up a 5th.)

Lionel Grigson is a pianist and teacher whose interest in jazz dates from his schooldays during the 1950s. From 1960 to 1963 he co-led the award-winning Cambridge University Jazz Band. He has subsequently performed with a number of leading American and British jazz artists including Freddie Hubbard, Philly Joe Jones, Johnny Griffin, Kenny Clark, Joe Harriott and Tubby Hayes, as well as leading his own bands. He currently teaches harmony and improvisation at the Guildhall School of Music and Drama. He is the author of A *Jazz Chord Book* (1981) and of *Practical Jazz* (1988).

Foreword

Charlie Parker's central position in the development of jazz is widely recognised, yet it can be very difficult for the student to find a way into the style. By setting forth a manageable number of Parker's themes and improvisations, with an analysis in relation to the harmonic foundation, it is hoped that this study album will remove some of the difficulties.

Solo transcriptions have become an established means of studying jazz. However, the desired result – to improve one's own improvisation – is not achieved simply by sight-reading. It is necessary to understand why the notes and phrases of a transcription were chosen in the first place. The best use of this Parker offering will be made by considering the relationship between the solos and the chord sequences on which they are based.

The six pieces in this study album have been chosen from the thirty-odd Parker copyrights available to the publisher. The selection is intended to illustrate the main forms within which Charlie Parker composed and improvised: the 12-bar blues and the 32-bar standard song form.

The chord sequence of *Au Privave* represents the standard 'modern jazz' (bebop) blues. *Moose the Mooche* and *Scrapple from the Apple* are based on closely-related versions of the AABA 32-bar form (in which the 8-bar A sections are harmonically nearly identical while B is a contrasting 'middle 8').

Ornithology is based on another common variant of the 32-bar form, the ABAC structure.

The chord sequence for *Blues for Alice* is a widely-used variation on the standard modern blues (e.g. *Au Privave*). The first four bars of the *Alice* sequence are shared by *Confirmation*, which is another example of the 32-bar AABA form.

In short, the core repertoire of jazz as developed by bebop really consists of variants of a few prototypical forms. If the beginner keeps this in mind, the essential task of *memorising* a large repertoire should become less daunting. The student who memorises the six themes and chord sequences in this collection will be well prepared for this task.

LIONEL GRIGSON

A Brief Biography

Charlie Parker was born on 29 August 1920 in Kansas City. His father, Charles Parker Sr, drifted away in the late 1920s and he was then brought up single-handed by his mother, Addie, who worked as a charwoman and took in lodgers to support herself and her son.

At 13, Parker showed interest in the radio performances of Rudy Vallee, a popular saxophonist, and his mother bought him a second-hand alto saxophone for $45. It was barely playable and his interest soon subsided. But at 15 he joined the marching band at Lincoln High School, first on alto horn then on baritone horn, under the noted bandmaster Alonzo Lewis. He became friendly with Lewis's older pupils, including the pianist Lawrence Keyes, and took up the alto saxophone again to join Keyes's band, the Deans of Swing.

Parker now became obsessively interested in music, but showed little promise at first. He suffered a famous humiliation when he tried to join in a jam session led by Count Basie's drummer Jo Jones. Jones expressed his disapproval of Parker's efforts by throwing his cymbal on the floor. In 1937 Parker played a summer season with vocalist George Lee's band. The pianist, Carrie Lee, and guitarist, Efferge Ware, taught him chords and key relationships.

Parker's musical development was now rapid. Two important influences were the alto saxophonist Buster Smith and Lester Young, tenor saxophone star with the Count Basie band. He bought Young's records with Basie, slowed them down to half-speed on a wind-up record player, and memorised Young's solos note-for-note.

By about this time, Parker had become a confirmed heroin addict. Possibly the knowledge that his addiction would eventually prove fatal drove him to apply himself to music with a single-minded intensity. A Faustian tragedy was in the making.

In 1938 he went to Chicago and then to New York. There, he washed dishes in a restaurant where the resident pianist was Art Tatum, technically and harmonically the most advanced jazz musician of the time. In jam sessions with a guitarist, Biddy Fleet, Parker practised chord extensions and achieved a break-through in learning how to integrate them into his melodic line. He then returned to Kansas City for his father's funeral, and afterwards briefly joined Harlan Leonard's band.

In 1939 Parker joined a fine Kansas City aggregation, the Jay McShann band, with which he worked semi-regularly for the next three and a half years.

In 1941 Parker returned to New York with the McShann band. With a few like-minded musicians – Dizzy Gillespie (trumpet), Thelonious Monk (piano), Kenny Clark (drums) – he consolidated his musical experimentations in jam sessions at Minton's Playhouse. Out of these sessions the revolutionary jazz style coalesced which became known as bebop.

He continued working with big bands (Earl Hines, Billy Eckstine) until 1944, when he formed a quintet with Dizzy Gillespie for a residency at the Three Deuces Club on New York's 52nd Street. This was the first regular bebop group.

In December 1945, together with Gillespie, Parker went to Hollywood for a two-month engagement at Billy Berg's club. He remained in California in 1946, where he recorded some historic sessions for Dial Records, then suffered a breakdown and was hospitalised for six months.

Temporarily restored to health, Parker returned to New York in April 1947, and formed a quintet with trumpeter Miles Davis (with whom he had recorded in California). He was now a celebrity and the acknowledged leader of the new jazz movement. The next few years were a period of increasing success and international recognition. However, he was living on borrowed time, the California hospitalisation having brought only a temporary respite from his addiction.

In 1949 Parker played at the Paris International Jazz Festival. On his return to New York he reformed his quintet with Red Rodney (trumpet). A new club, Birdland, was opened in his honour.

He reached his peak of commercial success in 1951, working steadily with his quintet and also with a string orchestra. He was now settled with his fourth wife, Chan Parker, by whom he had two children.

However, Parker's attempts to support his family were hampered by the loss of his cabaret card, which meant that he was unable to work in New York clubs. Though this was eventually restored, the early 1950s were a temporary plateau. In 1954, depressed by the death of his daughter from pneumonia, and beset by other problems, Parker attempted suicide and was again hospitalised. After this he temporarily rallied, but by 1955 he had entered a final decline. He died, aged 34, at the New York apartment of Baroness Nica de Koenigswater, on 12 March 1955.

The Style of Charlie Parker

'Intellectually bebop was so fascinating and tremendous and Charlie Parker was the most intellectual of them all. The music had such high spirit. The intensity, the sensitivity of the music was just fabulous.' (Red Rodney)*

'The most complex aspect of bop lies in the ingenuity with which the melodic line was originated . . . it breaks up into a large number of precisely thought-out phrases, each of which is an idea in its own right and may also be used in conjunction with any of the other phrases and on any tune whose chord structure is chromatic or diatonic. This may be compared to a jigsaw puzzle which can be put together in hundreds of ways . . .' (Lennie Tristano)**

Red Rodney (trumpet player with Parker's final regular quintet) pinpoints the combination of spirit and intellect which is the essence of Parker's style. The comments by Tristano (the leading jazz teacher of the 1940s) are a perceptive analysis of Parker's improvising method.

The foundation stone of Parker's music is the blues, which he absorbed in the rich musical environment of prohibition Kansas City in the 1930s. Parker's early employer Jay McShann (himself a formidable blues pianist) considered him to be the greatest of blues players. Some examples of Parker's pure blues phrasing in these transcriptions are *Au Privave* solo, third chorus, bars 4-7, and third chorus, bars 1-3; and *Blues for Alice* solo, first chorus, bars 4-7, and third chorus, bars 5-7.

Many of Parker's ideas are cadential, moving over chords II7 and V7 to chord I (e.g. in C: Dm7 G7 CΔ). Of course such movements occur in earlier jazz, but Parker seems to be the first wind player in jazz to use them systematically in improvisation. Two tunes of the 1920s must have prompted this thinking in the teenage Parker: Fats Waller's *Honeysuckle Rose*, and (also recorded by Waller), *Tea for Two*. The former was the first tune that Parker is said to have memorised.

The first phrase of *Honeysuckle Rose* is harmonised by the II–V change:

The *Honeysuckle* motif

One imagines the teenage Parker practising soloing on this number by starting with this phrase (or the first phrase for *Tea for Two*) and asking himself "How can I change this phrase, and where can I go from here?"

*from Ira Gitler, *Swing to Bop* (OUP 1985)
**from Robert George Reisner, *Bird: The Legend of Charlie Parker* (Citadel Press 1962)

Parker quite often uses variations and transpositions of the *Honeysuckle* motif wherever the context of a chord sequence allows. See *Scrapple* solo, bar 25; *Blues for Alice* theme, bar 8, also solo, second chorus, bar 8.

Together with Parker's use of II–V or II–V–I chord movements goes his highly practised skill in transposing ideas on these changes (and on individual chords) to any key, and therefore his ability to modulate to any key that presents itself in the course of a tune. No earlier jazz musician, except Art Tatum, has Parker's ability to play over challenging changes. His practice vehicle for these skills was another favourite tune, Ray Noble's *Cherokee*, with its middle section of descending II–V–I modulations (and punishing tempo):

The *Cherokee middle*:

(Key B♭) D♭m7 | G♭7 | BΔ | BΔ | Bm7 | E7 | AΔ | AΔ |

Am7 | D7 | GΔ | GΔ | Gm7 | C7 | Cm7 | F7+ || (to last 16 bars)

Apart from his use of cadence and modulation, the innovative feature in Parker's melodic line is its imaginative use of extended and other 'colour tones' to supplement the basic chord tones of root, 3rd, 5th and 7th, particularly over dominant 7th-type chords.

The 'normal' extensions of a dominant 7th chord are the 9th, 11th and 13th obtained by extending the chord upwards through the major scale of which it is the dominant:

G7 *as* V *of* C *major*

Parker was fond of the effect of the augmented 11th (+11) on dominant-type harmony. This extension results from interpreting a dominant 7th-type chord as chord IV7 of an ascending melodic minor scale:

G7 *as* IV7 *of* D *minor melodic (ascending)*

For an example of Parker's use of the augmented 11th, see *Moose the Mooche* solo, bars 17-19 (first three bars of middle).

Two other ways of obtaining interesting combinations of 'colour tones' on dominant harmony are obtained by locating the chord either in a diminished scale, or on the leading note of an ascending melodic minor.

G7 *as* I *of diminished scale (alternate semitones and tones)*

G7 (♭5) *on leading note of* A♭ *melodic minor (ascending)*

Both these scales provide G7 with two altered 9ths – one flat, the other sharp (♭9 and +9). Parker often places both these 9ths in a triplet or quaver-and-two-semiquaver turn on the dominant (see *Au Privave* solo, last chorus, bar 10).

The diminished scale also provides a regular 13th and an augmented 11th (+11).

In the A♭ minor melodic (ascending) scale, G7 has, apart from the two altered 9ths (flat and sharp), two altered 5ths, flattened and augmented (♭5 and +). (The + can also be described as a flat 13th). The major 3rd of G7 (B) is enharmonically equivalent to the minor 3rd (C♭) of A♭ minor.

Another way to describe the relationships between the dominant chord and the various combinations of additional notes is to run the added notes together with the basic chord tones to form a mental scale from the root of the chord (the basis of much jazz teaching in the USA and elsewhere – e.g. by George Russell and J. Aebersold).

The resulting scales are modes of the diatonic scales in which the chord can be diatonically located.

So for G7 as V7 of C major we get:

For G7 as IV7 of D melodic minor (ascending):

(This is sometimes called the 'Lydian Dominant' scale. It is the fourth mode of the melodic minor (ascending) scale.)

For G7+, or ♭5, on the leading note of A♭ melodic minor (ascending):

(This is sometimes called the 'Altered Dominant' or 'Diminished-Augmented' scale. It is the last (seventh) mode of the melodic minor (ascending).)

We do not know exactly how Charlie Parker thought about these relationships, i.e. whether he thought in terms of chords plus extensions, or scales on chords, or (most likely) some of both.

In some instances he is clearly thinking in scale terms. For example, bar 8 of his first solo chorus in *Au Privave* is (except for the last note) virtually a downwards G harmonic minor scale, played over its chords II7 and V7 (Aø and D7).

Simple chromatic notes, which need not be 'justified' in any chordal/scalar way, also enter into many of Parker's phrases (e.g. *Au Privave* solo, first chorus, bar 7).

Altogether, Parker's choice of notes illustrates the old dictum that any note will 'fit' a chord, provided you know how to resolve it. For students of jazz improvisation on chord changes, 'how' is the difficult question. This is where a detailed study of Parker's style and musical thought is valuable,

As much attention should be given to Parker's rhythm as to his choice of notes. The two aspects work together to throw a phrase into an unexpected relief, keeping the listener pleasantly off-balance. Parker's powerful swing is reinforced by his use of contrasting accentuation of strong and weak pulses. This works at several levels: the beat itself, half-beats and quarter-beats. A particular effect of some phrases is to dislocate the harmonic rhythm by seeming to make a new chord fall just before or after it is expected (see *Ornithology* solo, last chorus, bars 31-2).

Apart from the detailed content, both harmonic and rhythmic, of Parker's phrases, it is the overall architecture of the solos which commands admiration. On this point, the French critic André Hodeir makes a telling comment: 'Parker definitely seems to have been the first to bring off the difficult feat of introducing into jazz a certain melodic discontinuity that yet avoids incoherence.' *

One can conclude by saying that Parker's great skill is in generating a constantly fresh and varied melodic line which, though improvised, has the quality of a detailed, finished composition – and which should be the envy of almost any composer.

The Transcriptions and How to Use Them

Following Parker's own method of studying his major influence, Lester Young, these transcriptions were prepared by slowing down the taped recordings to half-speed (an octave lower than the original pitch) so that each note could be exactly checked. (Pete Burden, a fine saxophonist with a good ear for Parker, has kindly checked some of the harder double-time phrases.)

By all means play through the themes and solos as if they were any other notated compositions. But this is not the main purpose of using jazz transcriptions, which is to learn how to improvise by example. Memorise the themes and chord sequences, but not necessarily entire solos. Choose certain phrases, analyse them in relation to the underlying chord(s) and memorise them. Refer to the section, 'Selected Phrases', where typical Parker phrases have been collected together and classified. Phrases over II–V and II–V–I movements can be practised in every key. This will prepare you to improvise over these changes when they occur in other tunes and keys. There is nothing wrong in including a few verbatim Parker phrases in your own improvisations, where the context (chords) will allow. Develop your own variations of these borrowings.

It is essential to listen to the original recordings. Most of these are constantly duplicated in various issues and compilations and a little hunting in record shops or libraries should turn them up. In case of difficulty contact a specialist jazz shop such as Ray's Jazz Shop or Mole Jazz (London).

*from Robert George Reisner, *Bird: The Legend of Charlie Parker* (Citadel Press 1962)

Accompaniment

The chord sequences of most jazz tunes, including Parker's repertoire, are made up of five or six basic chord types. These are:

TYPE	CONVENTIONAL VOICING	SYMBOL
Major 7th		CΔ
Dominant 7th		C7
Minor 7th		Cm7
Half-diminished 7th		Cφ
Minor/major 7th		CmΔ
Diminished 7th		Co

For accompaniment, the simplest effective voicing of these chords (for piano or guitar) is to include only the root, 3rd and 7th and to leave out the 5th. On piano, the root should be in the LH and the 3rd and 7th in the RH. In this voicing, the minor 7th also serves for the half-diminished, reducing the chord list to five types.

This procedure is known as 'fewest notes' voicing. If we add to it the idea of voice-leading by 'least movement', a II–V–I sequence can be played as:

Dm7   G7   CΔ   Dm7   G7   CΔ

This combination of voicing and voice-leading can be summed up as the 'fewest notes, least movement' principle. It can be effectively applied to most jazz chord sequences, including those in this collection.

For the sake of the bass line, 1st and 2nd inversions are sometimes called for. These are indicated by writing the chord symbol over the appropriate bass note: $\frac{F7}{A}$ $\frac{F7}{C}$

    1st inv   2nd inv

The chord voicings in the written-out piano parts are based on the 'fewest notes, least movement' principle, but with one or more extensions (9th, 11th, 13th) sometimes added, as well as augmented or flattened 5ths where appropriate. The voicings approximate those played by Parker's preferred pianists – Duke Jordan, Al Haig – on the original recordings, but are not exact transcriptions. Haig's style of chordal accompaniment ('comping') is well described by Ross Russell: 'Haig does not play equal-time piano, or steady fours . . . His chords are well chosen, voiced and shaded, and worked into the texture of the rhythm section of which he is a part.'*

Chord intervals to be raised are preceded by a + sign. (By itself + means an augmented 5th.) Intervals to be lowered are preceded by a ♭ sign. A dominant symbol followed by 'sus 4' means that the 3rd is replaced by a suspended 4th.

The scored piano chords are written in 'equal time', i.e. as on-the-beat white notes, but the accompanist should of course vary the rhythmic positioning of the chords to achieve an authentic 'comping' style (as the above description of Haig's style suggests).

The piano parts are intended to fit the themes, but will usually suit the solos as well. Sometimes (e.g. in *Ornithology*) there are slight differences between the chord sequence of the theme and the sequence played for improvisation.

Pianists wishing to play these transcriptions will need to voice a left-hand accompaniment. Actually, a single-note bass line formed from the bottom notes of the written chords will suffice. Over this, the 3rd and 7th (or alternatively, the 7th and 3rd) can be added to complete the basic harmony. For those unable to stretch the left-hand voicing of the root, 7th and 3rd (i.e. spanning a 10th), either the root or the 3rd (10th) can be left out.**

Transcription Discography

Recording dates and personnels, in chronological order:

Moose the Mooche, Hollywood, 28 March 1946
Parker (alto saxophone), Miles Davis (trumpet), Lucky Thompson (tenor saxophone), Dodo Marmarosa (piano), Arvin Garrison (guitar), Vic McMillan (bass), Roy Porter (drums)
Available on 'Bird' Symbols, Charlie Parker Records PLP-407 and *Charlie Parker on Dial*, Vol.1, Spotlite Records 101

Scrapple from the Apple, New York, 4 November 1947
Parker, Davis, Duke Jordan (piano), Tommy Potter (bass), Max Roach (drums)
Available on *Memorial Charlie Parker*, Vogue CLD.753 (another version is on the 'Bird' Symbols album)

Au Privave, New York, 17 January 1951
Parker, Davis, Walter Bishop (piano), Teddy Kotick (bass), Max Roach (drums)
Available on *Swedish Schnapps* (*The Genius of Charlie Parker* # 8), Verve V6-8010

Blues for Alice, New York, 8 August 1951
Parker, Red Rodney (trumpet), John Lewis (piano), Ray Brown (bass), Kenny Clarke (drums)
Also on *Swedish Schnapps* album (see above)

Confirmation, New York, 4 August 1953
Parker, Al Haig (piano), Percy Heath (bass), Max Roach (drums)
Available on *Now's the Time* (*The Genius of Charlie Parker* # 3), Verve/Polydor 2304095 Mono

Ornithology, Boston, 22 September 1953
Parker, Red Garland (piano), Bernie Griggs (bass), Roy Haynes (drums)
Available on *Charlie Parker at Storyville*, Blue Note BT 85108

*from Ross Russell, *Bird Lives!* (Quartet Books 1973)
**For further information on chord voicings, see Lionel Grigson, *Practical Jazz* (Stainer & Bell, 1988).

Notes on Themes and Solos

(The phrases referred to here as a), b), etc, are marked accordingly in the transcriptions.)

1. AU PRIVAVE (1951)

Form: 12-bar blues

THEME

This optimistic, medium up-tempo theme is a fairly typical Parker blues head, strung together from a series of short melodic/rhythmic motifs which form an almost continuous 12-bar phrase. Bars 1-3 are a strong tonic statement in the major key, ignoring the usual subdominant chord in bar 2 of a blues. The opening statements of Parker's blues heads are often like this, close to the major triad and including the leading note rather than the flat 7th of the blues scale. The flat 7th (E♭) is saved, as in an old blues, for the fourth bar, to herald the coming sub-dominant.

In his blues themes, Parker's most overt blues statements, using the notes of the blues scale, are sometimes reserved for subdominant chords of bars 5 and 6 – as in *Au Privave* and the other blues in this collection, *Blues for Alice*.

Notice the positive rhythmic structure of each motif, and the use of syncopation to charge certain notes. Bars 1 and 2 imply a cross-metre of 3+3+2 beats against the **4/4** measure. The figure in bar 5 has the same pattern, 3+3+2, but in quavers. This is also the main rhythmic figure (bar 1 etc.) of *Moose the Mooche*.

SOLO – *three choruses (36 bars)*

FIRST CHORUS

a) This phrase sits on bars 2 and 3, i.e. in the middle of the first four bars rather than at the beginning. Once again the subdominant is ignored in favour of a clear tonic statement. The melody from bar 2 beat 2 to bar 3 beat 2 is an exact transposition of the first five beats of the *Ornithology* theme – but commencing on a weak instead of a strong beat. The last note of the whole phrase anticipates by 1½ beats the expected flat 7th of bar 4. Parker also uses this anticipation – the 'early 7th' – in the solos on *Blues for Alice* (first chorus, bar 3) and *Confirmation* (first chorus, bar 27).

b) Two short motifs, each with a pick-up of four semiquavers, over the subdominant in bars 5 and 6. The second motif is almost a repeat of the first, but with D♭, implying the subdominant minor, instead of D.

c) Nearly 4½ bars long, this phrase sits across the division between the second and last four bars of the chorus. It is constructed by running together two 'approach phrases' – first to the supertonic chord (Gm7, bar 9) and then, without pause, continuing to bar 11.

Bar 7 is the archetypal 'bop break', a quaver-and-triplet ascent from the leading note through the tonic triad, followed by a chromatic descent from the leading note (compare the break to solo starting in bar 31 of the *Ornithology* theme).

Bar 8 illustrates a standard Parker approach to the supertonic chord (in this key, Gm7) to commence the last four bars of a blues. Except for its last note, this bar is virtually a descending G harmonic minor scale, played over its II7 and V7 chords (Aφ and D7). (For another kind of supertonic approach, see *Blues for Alice* solo, second chorus, bar 8.)

Embedded in bar 9 (notes 2-5) is a quaver-and-triplet ascent like that in bar 7, but transposed to start on the 9th of Gm7. In bars 10 and 11 the line is built around a rising movement from the 5th to the augmented 5th of the dominant (C7) to the 3rd of the key (F).

SECOND CHORUS

d) A brief statement strongly and charmingly reaffirming the tonic, at the same time emphasising the **4/4** measure by placing obvious chord tones (root and 5th) on beats 1 and 3 of bar 1.

e) A long, winding 5-bar phrase, commencing with a three-quaver pick-up in bar 2 and approaching bar 5 (subdominant) in a generally downwards fashion, continuing through bars 5 and 6 to return to the tonic in bar 7. From the pick-up through bars 3 and 4, the choice of notes in relation to the chords disturbs the metre in a way not easy to analyse. Starting from the fourth beat of bar 2, the notes seem to arrange themselves in three bars of **3/4**. The line resolves onto B♭7 (bar 5) to continue with a bold upward design including the flat 9th (B), augmented 11th (E) and 13th (G), before returning in a straightforward way to the tonic.

f) Four beats' rest precedes the four-semiquaver pick-up to a Parker speciality – the double-time 'corkscrew' over Gm7 and C7 to F. The corkscrew effect is over the first half-bar of Gm7 (bar 9):

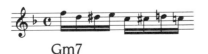

Gm7

Though Parker often uses this device, he always keeps the

listener guessing as to its continuation. In this case, he carries on the double-time through the rest of the bar and through the following bar (C7), using effective chromaticism (+5 and ♭9) in the second half of the bar, before resolving the phrase to the 5th of the tonic on bar 11.

THIRD CHORUS

g) Parker embellishes the last two bars of the second chorus with a couple of graceful flourishes which lead without pause to a down-to-earth blues statement over bars 1-3 – actually the first use of blue notes (flat 5th and flat 3rd of the blues scale) so far in this solo.

h) A three-note pick-up in bar 4, from an anticipated 9th on F7, leads to a downwards phrase through the subdominant (B♭7), which is effectively cut short on the last beat of bar 5. After two beats' rest a slow triplet motif (implying the subdominant minor) leads us back to the tonic (bar 7). Despite the rest between them the two parts of this phrase form one overall idea.

i) Another approach phrase to the supertonic (compare bar 8 with the same bar in the first chorus), resting after the first beat of bar 9. The whole phrase is made to sound as if it could be a beat late – if it began a beat earlier it would naturally end on the last beat of bar 8 (with the final quaver an anticipation of the next downbeat).

j) After 1½ beats' rest a three-quaver pick-up leads to the dominant (C7) in bar 10, on the first beat of which Parker sounds both the flat and sharp (augmented) 9th in a triplet turn, continuing into bar 11. The resolution of the phrase is delayed to the third beat, after suggesting an interpolated IV minor in the first half-bar.

k) A simple 'sign-off' phrase leading over the end of the chorus into the next.

2. SCRAPPLE FROM THE APPLE (1947)

Form: AABA 32 bars

An alternative take of this early quintet version. The chord changes to the A sections are basically those of Fats Waller's *Honeysuckle Rose* (a tune Parker recorded as a teenager), while the B section (middle 8) changes are those of the *I Got Rhythm* middle (transposed to F).

The *Scrapple* changes are therefore a hybrid of two basic AABA chord sequences.

THEME

The first four bars are a fair example of Parker's phrase composition over chords II7 and V7 in the major key. Notice how in bar 1 the major and flat 7ths (F♯ and F natural) are both used on II7 (Gm7), and how the flat 7th resolves (after a downward 3rd) to the 5th instead of the more usual 3rd of the dominant (C7) in the next bar. Bar 3 ends with an anticipated and unresolved flat 9th to C7.

Like most Parker themes, the *Scrapple* head is strongly rhythmic and can be played as a drum solo.

The middle 8 is improvised. Phrase *a*) negotiates two bars of A7 and a bar and one beat of D7. The flat and sharp 9th are sounded on the second beat of bar 17. The C♯ at the beginning of bar 19 seems like a wrong note, but 'belongs' to the A7 of the previous bar.

Phrase *b*) of the middle is a brief but triumphal double-time ascent to G7, reaching a high G which is effectively held from the last beat of bar 21 to the first beat of the next bar before descending to the 13th and 9th. A beat's rest precedes the semiquaver pick-up to phrase *c*), another example of the double-time 'corkscrew' over Gm7 and C7 (bars 23 and 24), with a pause before its final flourish.

SOLO – *one chorus* (32 *bars*)
FIRST 8

d), *e*) and *f*) The first 8 unfolds a series of three phrases of increasing length and complexity. The third and longest phrase, *f*), features characteristic passing chromaticism before leading to the beginning of the second 8. Notice, in the second half of bar 8, the oblique use of A♭m7, leading upwards through its 7th and 11th (G♭ and D♭) to the 5th (D) of the following chord (Gm7). (Compare *Ornithology* solo, first chorus, bar 14.)

SECOND 8

g) Double-time phrase from C7 back to Gm7. (Unusually for Parker, this seems slightly nervously executed.)

h) A fairly typical Parker approach from dominant to tonic (bars 12-13) which continues to suggest the second four bars of the I *Got Rhythm* changes rather than the regular *Scrapple* ones – i.e. moving to the subdominant in the next bar (bar 14) and then back in the next bar. The repeated turn in bars 14 and 15 suggests two bars of **3/4** starting on beat 2 of bar 14 (a cross-metre of 1+3+3+1 in place of 4+4 beats). This ending could be called the 'wiggle'.

MIDDLE 8

i) A classic negotiation of the first three bars of the *Rhythm* middle. The first two bars (17 and 18) are like a dominant approach to a tonic D on the third bar (19) – continuing, however, to the 7th. (Compare this bar to B*lues for Alice*, first chorus, bar 3.) Its ending gives this optimistic phrase a touch of pathos. If the forthcoming G7 is considered as the subdominant to D7, then the phrase ending has a similar meaning to the 'early' 7th in bar 3 of a blues.

j) A finely conceived 5-bar phrase leading to the first bar of the last 8. Bar 21 gets its harmonic sparkle from the use of the 13th and 9th together with the bright augmented 11th of G7.

LAST 8

k), *l*) and *m*) Not counting bar 25 (the ending of the previous phrase) the chorus concludes with three phrases of decreasing length, reversing the procedure of the first 8.

3. MOOSE THE MOOCHE (1946)
Form: AABA 32 bars ('Rhythm changes')
THEME

An early composition on the I *Got Rhythm* changes which is possibly Parker's most tightly organised theme. *Moose* is not easily memorised because of the differences between the first and second 8s and also because the middle 8 is composed rather than left open for improvisation. (Most 'rhythm heads' have nearly identical main 8s and thus one only really has to memorise 8 bars – the middle 8 being improvised.)

The primary motif is the rhythmic/melodic figure of bar 1 – another example of the 3+3+2 division of the bar, as in the *Au Privave* theme (bar 5). This rhythmic figure appears in the first and third bars of each main 8, as well as in bars 15 and 31, eight times in all.

The melodic/harmonic scheme of the first four bars of the main 8s reduces simply to I–V–I–V, and this is followed by a 'to subdominant and back' melody and progression in the second four. But the second four bars of the second 8 have a different 'subdominant and back' melody, and an ending tailored to lead to the middle 8 with an anticipated 9th on D7.

The middle 8 contrasts detached syncopations (bars 17, 20 and 24) with flowing quavers (bars 19, 21 and 22). Notice the use of 9ths and 13ths on D7 (bar 18) and G7 (bar 19); also the sharp and flat 9th on F7 (bar 24).

SOLO – *one chorus* (32 *bars*)

In contrast to the tightly-packed theme, the solo is organised in mostly longer phrases, with more rests.

FIRST 8

a) An opening statement centred around the tonic.

b) Starting on the same part of the bar as the previous phrase, but half-a-bar longer, this is a typical 'to IV and back' (via IV minor) phrase.

SECOND 8

c) A short tonic-to-dominant phrase occupying the first two bars only.

d) A long phrase (nearly five bars) sitting across the two four-bar sections of the second 8. Bars 11 and 12 approach the tonic in a generally downwards line; arriving at the tonic (bar 13) the phrase continues through bar 14 (IV and IVm) back to the tonic on bar 15.

Compare the phrase lengths and positions in these first two 8s. The first 8 consists of one phrase per four-bar section (symmetry). The second 8 contrasts this with a short phrase occupying the first two bars, followed by a long one across the four-bar sections (asymmetry).

MIDDLE 8

e) Following a quaver-and-triplet ascent (5th, 9th, natural 11th and 13th), the first chord (D7) of the middle 8 gets a favourite Parker effect, a descent from a 13th through an augmented 11th to a 9th and 7th, with 13th and augmented 11th repeated in the next bar (18). Notice how the augmented 11th effect is repeated on the next chord (G7, bar 19), though not by an exact transposition of the first motif.

f) This phrase approaches the dominant (F7) through its dominant (C7). With one chromatic passing note (Cb) the scale from the beginning of the phrase to the penultimate note of bar 21 is F melodic minor (ascending form played descending). Compare the phrase ending in bar 23 with the *Scrapple* solo, bar 19; the *Confirmation* solo, second chorus, bar 12; and this same solo, bar 30.

LAST 8

g) A simple, cheerful phrase reaffirming the tonic.

h) Like the second phrase (*d*)) of the second 8, this runs over the join between four-bar sections. Note the chromatic approach through Dm7 and Dbm7 in bar 27 to Cm7 (supertonic, bar 28), and the use of a simple Bb major scale over Cm7 and F7 in bar 28.

i) Signing off over the last bar into the next chorus.

4. ORNITHOLOGY (1953)

Form: ABAC 32 bars

THEME

The changes are derived, with one or two alterations to suit the new melody, from the song *How High the Moon*. The line should probably be co-credited to trumpeter Benny Harris, an early colleague.

The earliest version of *Ornithology* was recorded in 1946, at the same session (for Dial Records) that produced *Moose the Mooche* and the historic *Night in Tunisia*. In later versions, Parker dispensed with the across-the-band triplet-figure endings to the 16-bar sections of the original melody (which suited a three-horn front line), in favour of endings which were more convenient for one or two horns.

The changes commence with two bars of tonic (G) and then modulate downwards, first to F via Gm7 and C7, and then by the same move (II7 and V7 of the new key) to E♭. The landscape is therefore of a major scale turning minor, which is then revealed as the first step of the change to the new key, preparing its dominant.

Accordingly, Parker fashions first a bold major phrase (bar 1 to the first beat of bar 2), and then repeats its beginning in the minor, before revealing the true intention of this phrase (as shown by the high F) as the herald of F major. This key is then 'minored' to lead, via B♭7, to E♭ at bar 9. (To suit the melody, this chord should be E♭7, not E♭Δ, though this may be more convenient for improvisation.)

After E♭, the changes lead back to the tonic minor via its II7 and V7 (Aφ and D7). The last four bars of the second 8 are a 'double-length turnaround' (a bar each of Bm7, E7, Am7 and D7) to the third 8. The third 8 is a repeat of the first, and the last 8 shortens its turnaround to two bars, to arrive at the tonic at the last two bars — which Parker uses for a snappy break to his first solo chorus. (Compare the first bar of this break, bar 31, to the *Au Privave* solo, first chorus, bar 7.) Note the effective augmented 5th on the implied dominant (D7) in the second bar of this break.

SOLO – *three choruses* (96 *bars*)

In this live recording from a Boston club date, Parker is able to stretch out over a full three choruses. No phrase-by-phrase analysis is given, partly because of the length of the solo, but also because enough of the essential characteristics of Parker's style have so far been described in this collection to enable this magnificent solo to be understood without further commentary.

However, some selected highlights follow:

1. Bars 3 and 4 of the first chorus illustrate an interpretation of a 2-bar II–V movement, whereby Gm7 to C7 becomes Gm GmΔ| Gm7 C7, allowing the phrase to be built around the descending minim line G–F♯ –F natural–E.

2. Phrase *n*) is a surprising and rhythmically free quote of the first phrase of the song *Tenderly* (originally in **3/4** time).

3. The solo's climax, just after its mid-point, is the third 8 of the second chorus. This is heralded over bars 16 and 17 (over the ending of the second 8) by a precipitous downwards run from F natural (phrase *o*)). Phrase *p*) (bar 18) is a double-time feint over the tonic – and then Parker is off on a furiously intricate double-time 'corkscrew' (phrase *q*)), extending over Gm7 and C7 to a full bar of F, to end with what is almost a transposition of the first phrase of the theme.

4. Towards the end of the solo there is a remarkable 9-bar phrase (*z*)) of striking continuity, at first developing an apparent quotation, then leading to another transposed reference to the beginning of the theme at bar 25 (E♭).

5. BLUES FOR ALICE (1951)

Form: 12-bar blues ('Round the Clock')

THEME

The straight-ahead Au Privave was Parker's New Year blues for 1951 (recorded 17 January). The contrasting Blues for Alice was recorded eight months later, and is built on the variation of the blues changes variously known as the 'Bird blues', 'Swedish blues' or (in Britain) the 'Round the Clock' blues.

The simplest representation of the Alice changes, compared with the basic 'modern' blues changes, is:

```
BASIC                                    ALICE

F       |Bb7    |F     |F7     |         F       |A7    |Dm    |F7     |

Bb7     |Bb7    |F     |D7     |         Bb      |Bbm   |F     |Abo    |

Gm7     |C 7    |F  D7 |Gm7 C7 ||        Gm7     |C7    |F  D7 |Gm7 C7||
```

The main differences are in the first eight bars. In the first four, the Alice changes go to the relative minor in bar 3. In the second four, the return to the tonic is via IVm, and the approach to the supertonic is the diminished chord on III.

In a more schematised form (the strict 'Round the Clock' sequence) the Alice changes become:

```
FΔ      | Em7       A7    | Dm7    G7  |Cm7    F7   |
        | Eø

BbΔ     | Bbm7      Eb7   | Am7    D7  |Abm7   Db7  |

Gm7     | C7              | FΔ     D7  |Gm7    C7   ||
```

While the 'Round the Clock' scheme forms a suitable accompaniment to the theme, and solo, they can equally well be accompanied by the more basic changes given above (John Lewis, on piano, is closer to these at points). In other words, Parker does not depend on passing chords, and can pare down a sequence to its essential changes.

The trickiest modulation afforded by the Alice changes is that implied (but not fulfilled) in bar 8, by Abm7–Db7 (or either chord alone) to Gb major. Notice the melody at this point of the theme, and also the phrase at the same point in the second chorus of the solo — both are variants of the first phrase of Honeysuckle Rose, transposed up a semitone.

For the most part, the theme flows through the changes and is not blues-like; however, the last four notes of bar 4 and the whole of bar 5 are a heart-felt blues phrase (compare bar 5 of Au Privave).

SOLO – *three choruses (36 bars)*

FIRST CHORUS

a) Bar 1 emphasises the major 7th of the tonic on beats 1 and 3 (dissonance on strong beats), and bar 2 seems to head for the relative minor in a straightforward way. But in bar 3 Parker avoids the expected resolution and instead anticipates the chords of the next bar — another example of the 'early 7th'.

b) A heartfelt blues phrase over IV and IVm (bars 5 and 6) leading back to the tonic (or III7) in bar 7. The last three notes in this bar are the same as in bar 3, but this time with a different meaning — the final Eb anticipating the chords in bar 8.

c) A short phrase on the supertonic.

d) Another variation of the double-time 'corkscrew', this time commencing over V7 rather than II7.

SECOND CHORUS

e) A variation or development of the opening phrase *a*) of the first chorus, this time extended to bar 4. Bars 3 and 4 are occupied by two motifs each beginning with a turn, first suggesting D minor then subtly varied to suggest F7, and positioned so as to divide the two bars into 3+3+2 beats.

f) As in the previous chorus, this begins as a blues phrase over IV and IVm, and is extended to end with an ingenious transposition of a familiar idea to fit the chords of bar 8.

g) Double-time over II–V–I. The phrase seems to begin with a deliberate false start – as if Parker intends the listener to expect another 'corkscrew' but then breaks off to continue in a different way.

THIRD CHORUS

h) An expressively held note over the final bar of the previous chorus leads to a brief tonic figure on bar 1.

i) This phrase moves to the relative minor and then to the tonic 7th. Compare bar 2 with the same bar in the first two choruses – each has similar ingredients (basically a D harmonic minor scale), but are handled differently each time.

j) and *k*) are marked as separate phrases being separated by 1½ beats' rest, but taken together they are a blues-scale treatment of IV and IVm, as in the first two choruses.

l) Double-time II–V–I, as in the second chorus, and again with a 'deliberate false start' (but with different notes).

m) Held note into the last bar leading to a double-time sign-off into the next chorus.

SUMMARY

Altogether this seems like one of Parker's most carefully composed blues improvisations. Each chorus is built in four-bar episodes: the first four bars clearly outlining the change to the relative minor; the second four featuring a blues statement over the subdominant; and the last four featuring a double-time return to the tonic. This episodic similarity gives the whole solo an overall unity which, however, is balanced by a wealth of detailed variation between the corresponding episodes in each chorus.

6. CONFIRMATION (1953)

Form: AABA 32 bars

THEME

The changes to the first four bars of the main 8s are the same as the first four of *Blues for Alice*, i.e. essentially F–A7–Dm–F7, and so it is interesting to compare the two themes and also Parker's improvisations in these sections. The *Confirmation* changes continue like a foreshortened blues with a bar of the subdominant, then moving to a half-close in the first 8 and to a full-close in the second and last 8s. The middle 8 includes two modulations, first to the subdominant (B♭) and then to the flat submediant (D♭) (=flat mediant of subdominant), each new key being approached by its II–V. The eighth bar is II–V back to F.

Against the similar changes of the main 8s (second and last 8s identical, second 8 identical save for its last two bars), Parker has worked out a mostly through-composed theme, with little repetition of material. The only identical bars in the main 8s are bars 2 and 26, and 4–5 and 28–9. This is a far cry from a simple AABA head like *Scrapple from the Apple*, which is really only eight bars of music.

Nevertheless Parker unifies the theme by having partly similar bars (compare bars 1 and 25, last beats), and bars which are nearly inversions of each other (compare bars 5 and 13). The most obvious unifying device is in the way that the first phrases of each main 8, though beginning differently, end with the same three syncopated notes.

The first two bars of the middle 8 are based on the idea of dividing a bar each of Cm7 and F7 into half-bars of Cm – CmΔ – Cm7 – F7 to allow the descending minim line C-B-B♭-A.
The melody follows this outline, but flattens the expected A on beat 3 of bar 18 to an A♭ – the augmented 9th instead of the 3rd of F7. (Compare *Ornithology* solo, first chorus, bars 3-4.)

Note the intricate, tumbling line in bar 21 (E♭m7). Bar 23 (D♭Δ) is the last phrase of the Dizzy Gillespie composition *Woody 'n' You*, played double-time.

SOLO – *two choruses (64 bars)*
No analysis is given, for the same reasons that none was given for the *Ornithology* solo. Both these solos are masterpieces, showing Parker at the height of his autumnal powers.

Selected Phrases

A. DOUBLE-TIME PHRASES

1. CORKSCREWS

i) *Scrapple* (1947), middle, phrase *c*), bars 23 and 24

ii) *Au Privave* (1951), second chorus, phrase *f*), bars 9-11

iii) *Blues for Alice* (1951), first chorus, phrase *d*), bars 10 and 11

iv) *Ornithology* (1953), second chorus, third 8, phrase *q*), bars 19-22

2. OTHER DOUBLE-TIME PHRASES

i) *Scrapple*, first chorus, middle 8, phrase *b*), bars 21 and 22

Solo, second 8, phrase *g*), bars 10 and 11

ii) *Blues for Alice*, second chorus, phrase *g*), bars 9-11 (the 'false start')

Third chorus, phrases *l*) and *m*), bars 9-11

iii) *Ornithology*, first chorus, third 8, phrase *g*), bars 20-22

iv) *Confirmation*, first chorus, second 8, phrase *d*), bars 10-12

B. DOMINANT EXTENSION & ALTERATION

i) Augmented 5th, rising

Au Privave, first chorus

ii) Augmented 5th, falling

Au Privave, second chorus

iii) Flat 9 and sharp 9

Au Privave, third chorus

iv) Augmented 11th (with 13 and 9)

Scrapple, middle 8

Moose the Mooche, middle 8

v) Dominant 'altered' (+9, ♭9, +5)

Ornithology, second chorus

C. BLUES PHRASES

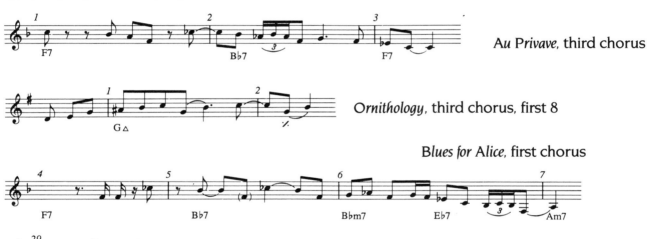

Au Privave, third chorus

Ornithology, third chorus, first 8

Blues for Alice, first chorus

Confirmation, last chorus

D. SCALAR PASSAGES

harmonic minor (Gm)

Au Privave, first chorus

major (B♭)

Moose the Mooche, last 8

major (F)

Ornithology, theme, bar 3

'harmonic major' (F)

Blues for Alice, second chorus, bar 10

E. ARPEGGIATION

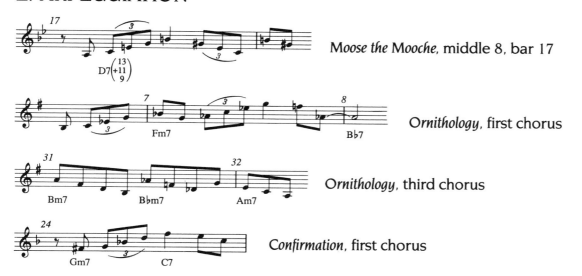

Moose the Mooche, middle 8, bar 17

Ornithology, first chorus

Ornithology, third chorus

Confirmation, first chorus

F. RHYTHMIC/METRIC DEVICES

1. SYNCOPATION

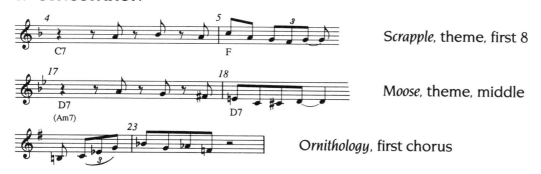

Scrapple, theme, first 8

Moose, theme, middle

Ornithology, first chorus

2. CROSS-METRE

Au Privave, theme

Vorwort

Die zentrale Stellung Charlie Parkers in der Entwicklung der Jazzmusik ist in weiten Kreisen anerkannt, dennoch kann es dem Lernenden schwerfallen, einen Zugang zu seinem Stil zu finden. Wir hoffen, daß dieses Übungsbuch einige Schwierigkeiten beseitigen wird, indem eine überschauliche Anzahl von Parkerschen Themen und Improvisationen mit einer Analyse der harmonischen Grundlage dargelegt wird.

Bei der Auseinandersetzung mit der Jazzmusik sind Solotranskriptionen zu einem anerkannten Hilfsmittel geworden. Doch wird das gewünschte Ergebnis, nämlich die Weiterentwicklung der eigenen Improvisationen, nicht dadurch erreicht, indem man die Transkriptionen einfach vom Blatt spielt. Man muß verstehen, warum die Töne und die Phrasen eines Stückes überhaupt gewählt wurden. Daher wird man vom Studium dieser Sammlung am meisten profitieren, wenn man die Beziehung zwischen den Solos und den ihnen als Basis dienenden Akkordfolgen beachtet.

Die sechs Stücke in diesem Übungsbuch sind von den über 30 urheberrechtlich geschützten Werken Parkers, die dem Verleger zur Verfügung standen, entnommen. Die Auswahl soll die Hauptformen, in denen Charlie Parker komponierte und improvisierte, veranschaulichen: Nämlich die Form des 12taktigen Blues und die der 32taktigen klassischen Liedform.

Die Akkordfolge in *Au Privave* stellt die herkömmliche 'moderne Jazzmusik', den (Bebop) Blues dar. *Moose the Mooche* und *Scrapple from the Apple* basieren auf engverwandten Versionen der AABA 32taktigen Form (in der die 8taktigen A-Teile harmonisch fast identisch sind, während B eine kontrastierende "Mitte-8" ist).

Ornithology basiert auf einer anderen oft vorkommenden Variante der 32taktigen Form, der ABAC-Struktur.

Die Akkordfolge für *Blues for Alice* ist eine oft verwendete Variation des klassischen modernen Blues (z.B. *Au Privave*). Die ersten vier Takte der *Alice*- Akkordfolge kommen auch in *Confirmation* vor, die ein weiteres Beispiel der 32taktigen AABA-Form ist.

Kurz gesagt, das Kernrepertoir der Jazzmusik, wie sie durch den Bebop entwickelt wurde, besteht in der Tat aus den Varianten einiger Urformen. Wenn der Anfänger dies im Gedächtnis behält, müsste die durchaus notwendige Arbeit des Auswendiglernens eines großen Repertoires ihm weniger entmutigend erscheinen. Der Lernende, der die Satzthemen und Akkordfolgen in dieser Sammlung auswendig lernt, wird für diese Aufgabe gut vorbereitet sein.

LIONEL GRIGSON

Kurze Biographie

Charlie Parker wurde am 29.8.1920 in Kansas City geboren. Sein Vater, Charlie Parker sen., trennte sich von der Familie in den späten zwanziger Jahren. Danach wurde er von seiner Mutter, Addie, allein erzogen; sie arbeitete als Putzfrau und vermietete Zimmer, um den Lebensunterhalt für sich und ihren Sohn zu sichern.

Mit 13 Jahren zeigte Parker Interesse für die Rundfunkaufführungen von Rudy Vallee, einem beliebten Saxophonspieler, und seine Mutter kaufte ihm ein gebrauchtes Altsaxophon für $45. Es war kaum spielbar, und sein Interesse ließ bald nach. Aber mit 15 Jahren wurde er Mitglied der Blaskapelle der Lincoln High School und spielte unter der Leitung des bekannten Kapellmeisters Alonzo Lewis, zuerst Althorn, dann Tenorhorn. Er schloß Freundschaften mit älteren Schülern von Lewis, u.a. mit dem Pianisten Lawrence Keyes, und nahm wieder das Saxophonspiel auf, um Keyes Band, der 'Deans of Swing', beizutreten.

Parker war jetzt von der Musik besessen, aber zeigte zuerst wenig Talent. Er erfuhr eine mittlerweile berühmt gewordene Demütigung, als er an einer Jam-Session unter der Leitung von Count Basies Schlagzeuger Jo Jones teilzunehmen versuchte. Jones zeigte sein Mißfallen an Parkers Versuchen, indem er sein Becken zu Boden warf. Im Jahre 1937 spielte Parker während der Sommerspielzeit in der Jazzband des Sängers George Lee. Der Pianist, Carrie Lee, und der Gitarrenspieler Efferge Ware, lehrten ihn Akkorde und Tonartverwandtschaften.

Parkers musikalische Entwicklung ging jetzt schnell voran. Zwei wichtige Einflüsse waren der Altsaxophonspieler Buster Smith und Lester Young, Tenorsaxophon-Virtuose im Orchester von Count Basie. Parker kaufte Schallplatten mit Aufnahmen von Young und Basie, spielte sie mit halber Geschwindigkeit auf einem aufziehbaren Plattenspieler und lernte Ton für Ton Youngs Solopartien auswendig.

Ungefähr um diese Zeit war Parker schon heroinabhängig. Vielleicht war es das Wissen, daß seine Sucht sich eines Tages als tödlich erweisen würde, das ihn dazu trieb, sich der Musik mit zielbewußter Intensität zu widmen. Eine faustische Tragödie war im Entstehen begriffen.

1938 fuhr er nach Chicago, dann nach New York. Dort spülte er Geschirr in einem Restaurant, wo der Pianist Art Tatum regelmäßig auftrat, der vom Standpunkt der Technik und Harmonie der modernste Jazzmusiker der Zeit war. In Jam-Sessions mit einem Gitarrenspieler namens Biddy Fleet übte Parker Akkorderweiterungen und erreichte einen Durchbruch als er lernte, sie in seine melodische Linie einzubauen. Danach kehrte er zurück nach Kansas City, um an der Beerdigung seines Vaters teilzunehmen, und trat kurze Zeit dem Jazzorchester von Harlan Leonard bei.

Im Jahre 1939 wurde Parker Mitglied im sehr guten Jay McShann Jazzorchester in Kansas City, wo er in den folgenden dreieinhalb Jahren mehr oder weniger regelmäßig arbeitete.

Im Jahre 1941 kehrte Parker mit der McShann Band nach New York zurück. Mit ein paar gleichgesinnten Musikern – Dizzy Gillespie (Trompete), Thelonious Monk (Klavier) und Kenny Clark (Schlagzeug) – festigte er seine musikalischen Experimente in Jam-Sessions in Minton's Playhouse. Aus diesen Zusammenkünften entwickelte sich ein revolutionärer Jazzstil, der als Bebop bekannt wurde.

Parker arbeitete bis zum Jahre 1944 weiter mit Bigbands (Earl Hines, Billy Eckstine), bis er schließlich ein Quintett mit Dizzy Gillespie gründete, das regelmäßig im Three Deuces Club, 52nd St., New York, auftrat. Dies war die erste reguläre Bebop-Gruppe.

Im Dezember 1945 ging Parker wegen eines zweimonatigen Engagements im Billy Berg Club zusammen mit Gillespie nach Hollywood. 1946 blieb er in Kalifornien, wo er für Dial Records einige historische Jam-Sessions aufnahm. Dann aber erlitt er einen Zusammenbruch und mußte für sechs Monate ins Krankenhaus.

Vorübergehend wieder gesund, kehrte Parker im April 1947 nach New York zurück und gründete ein Quintett mit dem Trompeter Miles Davis (mit dem er Schallplattenaufnahmen in Kalifornien gemacht hatte). Er war jetzt eine berühmte Persönlichkeit und der anerkannte Führer der neuen Jazzbewegung. Die folgenden Jahre waren eine Zeit wachsenden Erfolges und zunehmender Anerkennung. Doch dies war nicht von Dauer; sein Krankenhausaufenthalt in Kalifornien hatte ihn nur vorübergehend von seiner Sucht befreit.

Im Jahre 1949 spielte Parker beim Internationalen Jazzfestival in Paris. Bei seiner Rückkehr nach New York formierte er erneut sein Quintett mit Red Rodney (Trompete). Einer neuer Klub, "Birdland" genannt, wurde ihm zu Ehren eröffnet. 1951 erreichte er den Höhepunkt seines kommerziellen Erfolgs während er regelmäßig mit seinem Quintett und einem Streichorchester arbeitete. Er war jetzt mit seiner vierten Frau, Chan Parker, verheiratet, mit der er zwei Kinder hatte.

Jedoch wurden Parkers Versuche, seine Familie zu unterhalten, durch den Verlust seiner Cabaret-Karte erschwert; dies bedeutete, daß er in den New Yorker Klubs nicht arbeiten konnte. Obgleich die Karte schließlich zurückgegeben wurde, waren die frühen fünfziger Jahre nur ein vorübergehender Höhepunkt. Im Jahre 1954, depremiert über den Tod seiner Tochter, die an einer Lungenentzündung starb, und von anderen Problemen bedrängt, unternahm Parker einen Selbstmordversuch und mußte wieder ins Krankenhaus. Danach erholte er sich vorübergehend, aber 1955 ging es mit seinen Kräften schnell abwärts. Er starb am 12.3.1955 im Alter von 34 Jahren in der Wohnung der Baronin Nica de Koenigswater in New York.

Der Stil Charlie Parkers

"Verstandesmäßig gesehen war Bebop so faszinierend und ungeheuerlich und Charlie Parker war von allen der Intellektuellste. Die Musik war von solch ausgelassener Heiterkeit, die Intensität, die Sensibilität der Musik war wirklich fabelhaft." (Red Rodney) (aus: Ira Gitler, *Swing to Bop, OUP 1985*)

"Der komplizierteste Aspekt von Bop liegt in der Findigkeit mit der die melodische Linie entstand. Sie löst sich auf in einer großen Anzahl sehr genau ausgedachter Phrasen, von denen jede eine Idee für sich ist, die auch in Verbindung mit allen anderen Phrasen und mit jeder Melodie, deren Akkordstruktur chromatisch oder diatonisch ist, angewendet werden kann. Dies kann man mit einem Puzzlespiel vergleichen, das auf hundertfache Weise zusammengesetzt werden kann . . ." (Lennie Tristano) (aus: Robert George Reisner, *Bird: The Legend of Charlie Parker*, Citadel Press, 1962).

Red Rodney (Trompeter im letzten regelmäßig spielenden Quintett von Parker) beschreibt genau die Kombination von Geist und Intellekt, die das Wesentliche an Parkers Stil ist. Die Bemerkungen von Tristano (dem führenden Jazzleader der vierziger Jahre) sind eine einsichtsvolle Analyse der Improvisationsmethode Parkers.

21

Der Grundstein von Parkers Musik ist der Blues, den er in der reichen musikalischen Umwelt von Kansas City in den dreißiger Jahren, als das Alkoholverbot galt, aufnahm. Parkers früherer Arbeitgeber, Jay McShann (der selbst ein sehr großer Bluesspieler auf dem Klavier war), hielt ihn für den größten Bluesmusiker. Einige Beispiele Parkers reiner Blues-Phrasierungen in diesen Transkriptionen sind *Au Privave* Solo, dritter Chorus, Takte 4-7 und dritter Chorus, Takte 1-3; und *Blues for Alice* Solo, erster Chorus, Takte 4-7, und dritter Chorus, Takte 5-7.

Viele von Parkers Ideen sind kadenzähnlich und führen über die Akkorde II7 und V7 zu Akkord I (z.B. in C-dur: Dm7 G7 CΔ). Natürlich kommen solche Akkordfolgen auch in der frühen Jazzmusik vor, aber Parker scheint der erste Bläser in der Jazzmusik zu sein, der sie systematisch beim Improvisieren anwendete. Zwei Melodien der zwanziger Jahre müssen diese Gedanken im Teenager Parker hervorgerufen haben: *Honeysuckle Rose* von Fats Waller und (auch von Waller aufgenommen) *Tea for Two*. Die erstgenannte ist die erste Melodie, die Parker auswendig gelernt haben soll.

Die erste Phrase von *Honeysuckle Rose* wird durch die II-V-Folge harmonisiert:

Das *Honeysuckle* Motiv

Man stellt sich den Teenager Parker vor, wie er sein Solo zu diesem Stück spielt, mit dieser Phrase (oder der ersten Phrase von *Tea for Two*) anfängt und sich fragt: "Wie kann ich diese Phrase ändern, und wie soll ich weiterspielen?"

Parker wendet Variationen und Transkriptionen des *Honeysuckle*-Motivs ziemlich oft an, dort wo der Kontext einer Akkordfolge es erlaubt. Siehe *Scrapple*-Solo, Takt 25; *Blues for Alice*-Thema, Takt 8, und Solo, 2. Chorus, Takt 8.

Parkers Gebrauch von II-V oder II-V-I-Akkordfolgen zusammen mit seiner sehr geübten Fertigkeit, Ideen über dieser Akkordfolge (und über Einzelakkorden) nach jeder Tonart zu transponieren, befähigen ihn, nach jeder Tonart, die sich im Verlauf einer Melodie ergibt, zu modulieren. Keine früheren Jazzmusiker, außer Art Tatum, haben Parkers Fähigkeit, über herausfordernden Akkordfolgen zu spielen. Das Stück, das er übte, um diese Fertigkeiten zu entwickeln, war eine andere beliebte Melodie, Ray Nobles *Cherokee*, mit seinem Mittelteil mit absteigenden II-V-I-Modulationen (und bestrafendem Tempo):

Der *Cherokee*-Mittelteil:

B-dur

| D♭m7 | G♭7 | HΔ | HΔ | Hm7 | E7 | AΔ | AΔ | |
| Am7 | D7 | GΔ | GΔ | Gm7 | C7 | Cm7 | F7+ | ‖ |

(soll 16 Takte dauern)

Außer seiner Art, Kadenzen und Modulationen anzuwenden, besteht der neuartige Grundzug in der melodischen Linie Parkers, in dem fantasievollen Gebrauch von erweiteren und anderen "Farbtönen", um die Grundakkordtöne, bestehend aus Akkordgrundton, Terz, Quinte und Septime, zu ergänzen, besonders über Akkorde vom Dominantseptakkord-Typ.

Die "normalen" Erweiterungen eines Dominantseptakkords sind die None, die Undezime und die Tredezime, die man durch Aufwärtserweiterung des Akkords durch die Dur-Tonleiter, dessen Dominante er ist, erhält:

G7 als V von C-dur

Parker liebte die Wirkung der übermäßigen Undezime (+11) auf eine Harmonie des Dominant-Typs. Diese Erweiterung entsteht daraus, daß man einen Akkord des Dominantsept-Typs als den Akkord IV7 einer aufsteigenden melodischen Moll-Tonleiter versteht:

G7 als IV7 von der melodischen Moll-Tonleiter von d-moll (aufsteigend)

Ein Beispiel für Parkers Gebrauch der übermäßigen Undezime findet sich in *Moose the Mooche*, Solo, Takte 17-19 (erste drei Takte des Mittelteils).

Interessante Kombinationen von "Farbtönen" über Dominant-Harmonien können noch auf zwei andere Arten hergestellt werden, indem man den Akkord entweder in eine verminderte Tonleiter oder ihn auf den

Leitton einer aufsteigenden melodischen Moll-Tonleiter setzt.

G7 als I von einer verminderten Tonleiter (alternierende Halbtöne und Ganztöne)

G7$^{(♭5)}$ Erniedrigungszeichen auf dem Leitton der melodischen as-moll-Tonleiter (aufsteigend)

Diese beiden Tonleitern stellen G7 zwei veränderte Nonen, die eine erniedrigt, die andere erhöht (♭9 und +9), zur Verfügung. Parker setzt diese beiden Nonen oft in einem aus einer Triole oder einem Achtel mit zwei Sechzehnteln bestehenden Doppelschlag auf die Dominante (siehe *Au Privave* Solo, letzter Chorus, Takt 10).

Die verminderte Tonleiter besitzt auch eine normale Tredezime und eine übermäßige Undezime (+11).

In der melodischen as-moll-Tonleiter (aufsteigend) hat G7, außer den zwei veränderten Nonen (der erniedrigten und erhöhten None) zwei veränderte Quinten, die verminderte und die übermäßige Quinte (♭5 und +). Den + kann man auch als verminderte Tredezime bezeichnen). Die Durterz von G7 (H) ist enharmonisch der Mollterz (C♭) von as-moll gleich.

Eine weitere Art, die Verwandtschaften zwischen Dominantakkord und den verschiedenen Kombinationen von zugefügten Tönen zu beschreiben ist, die zugefügten Töne mit den Grundakkordtönen zusammenzunehmen um eine "geistige" Tonleiter vom Grundton des Akkords zu bilden. (Dies ist sehr oft die Grundlage des Jazzunterrichts in den USA und anderswo – z.B. im Unterricht von George Russell und J. Aebersold).

Die daraus entstehenden Tonleitern sind Modi der diatonischen Tonleitern in die der Akkord diatonisch gesetzt werden kann.

Für G7 als V7 von C-dur haben wir:

Mixolydische Kirchentonart

Für G7 als IV7 der melodischen d-moll-Tonleiter (aufsteigend):

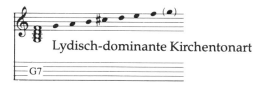
Lydisch-dominante Kirchentonart

(Dies wird manchmal die "Lydische Dominant-Tonleiter" genannt. Sie ist der vierte Modus der melodischen Moll-Tonleiter (aufsteigend)).

Für G7+, oder ♭5, auf dem Leitton von as-moll (melodisch, aufsteigend):

Dominant-alterierte Tonart

(Dies wird manchmal die "Alterierte Dominante" oder die "Verminderte-Vergrößerte Tonleiter" genannt. Sie ist der letzte, siebte Modus der melodischen Moll-Tonleiter (aufsteigend)).

Wir wissen nicht genau, wie Charlie Parker über diese Verwandtschaften dachte, ob er an Akkorde mit Erweiterungen oder an Tonleitern, die auf Akkorden aufgebaut sind, oder, was sehr wahrscheinlich ist, ob er an beides dachte.

In manchen Fällen denkt er offensichtlich an Tonleitern. Zum Beispiel Takt 8 seines ersten Solo-Chorus in *Au Privave* ist (außer der letzten Note) im Prinzip eine absteigende harmonische g-moll-Tonleiter, über den Akkorden II7 und V7 (A∅ und D7) gespielt.

Einfache, chromatische Töne, die nicht durch Akkorde oder "Tonleitern" gerechtfertigt werden müssen, kommen auch in vielen von Parkers Phrasen vor (z.B. im *Au Privave* Solo, 1. Chorus, Takt 7).

Im ganzen veranschaulicht Parkers Auswahl von Tönen den alten Ausspruch, daß jeder Ton zu jedem Akkord "paßt", solange man weiß, wie er aufzulösen ist. Für Studierende der Jazzimprovisation über Akkordfolgen ist dieses "Wie" die schwierige Frage. Hier kann ein eingehendes Studium von Parkers Stil und musikalischer Denkweise sehr wertvoll sein, um nicht zu sagen, unverzichtbar.

Man soll Parkers Rhythmus genausoviel Beachtung schenken wie seiner Tonauswahl. Die zwei Aspekte zusammen bewirken, daß der Zuhörer durch unerwartetes Hervorheben einer Phrase angenehm aus dem Gleichgewicht geworfen wird. Parkers gewaltiger Swingstil wird durch die kontrastierende Betonung starker und schwacher Schläge noch verstärkt. Diese Betonung wird entweder auf dem Schlag selbst oder auf Halb- und Viertelschlägen angewendet. Eine besondere Wirkung mancher Phrasen wird dadurch gewonnen, daß der harmonische Rhythmus verschoben wird, indem ein neuer Akkord früher oder später als erwartet folgt (siehe *Ornithology* Solo, letzter Chorus, Takt 31-2).

Außer dem harmonisch und rhythmisch detaillierten Inhalt von Parkers Phrasen ist es die gesamte Architektur der Soli, die Bewunderung hervorruft. Dazu macht der französische Kritiker André Hodeir eine vielsagende Bemerkung: "Parker scheint mit Sicherheit der erste gewesen zu sein, dem das schwierige Kunststück gelungen ist, in die Jazzmusik eine gewisse Zusammenhanglosigkeit hineinzubringen, die trotzdem die Unlogik vermeidet." (aus: Robert George Reisner, *Bird: The Legend of Charlie Parker,* Citadel Press 1962)

Abschließend kann man sagen, daß Parkers größte Fähigkeit darin liegt, eine immer wieder frische und variierte melodische Linie zu entwickeln, die, obgleich improvisiert, die Qualität einer genau ausgearbeiteten, fertigen Komposition besitzt, die jeder Komponist beneiden könnte.

Die Transkriptionen und ihre Anwendung

Parkers eigener Methode folgend, Lester Young, der ihn am meisten beeinflußte, zu studieren, wurden diese Transkriptionen vorbereitet, indem die Tonbandaufnahmen mit halber Geschwindigkeit gespielt wurden (eine Oktave tiefer als die originale Tonhöhe), so daß jeder Ton überprüft werden konnte. (Pete Burden, ein ausgezeichneter Saxophonspieler, der ein gutes Gehör für Parkers Musik hat, überprüfte freundlicherweise einige der schwierigen Phrasen, die in doppelten Notenwerten gespielt worden sind.)

Auf alle Fälle spielen Sie die Themen und Soli durch, als ob sie jede andere aufgezeichnete Komposition wären. Aber dies ist nicht das Hauptziel von Jazztranskriptionen; das Ziel ist vielmehr, daß man durch Beispiele zu improvisieren lernt. Lernen Sie Themen und Akkordfolgen, aber nicht unbedingt ganze Solostücke, auswendig. Wählen Sie bestimmte Phrasen, analysieren Sie im Verhältnis zu den darunterliegenden Akkorden und lernen Sie sie auswendig. Lesen Sie den Abschnitt "Ausgewählte Phrasen", wo typische Parkersche Phrasen gesammelt und klassifiziert worden sind. Phrasen über den Akkordfolgen II-V und II-V-I können in jeder Tonart geübt werden. Dadurch werden Sie darauf vorbereitet, mit diesen Akkordfolgen zu improvisieren, wenn sie in anderen Melodien und Tonarten vorkommen. Es ist nichts dagegen einzuwenden, ein paar Parkersche Phrasen unverändert in Ihre eigenen Improvisationen zu übernehmen, wenn der Zusammenhang (die Akkorde) dies erlaubt. Entwickeln Sie daraus Ihre eigenen Variationen.

Es ist unbedingt notwendig, Originalaufnahmen zu hören. Die meisten von diesen werden immer wieder in verschiedenen Ausgaben und Sammlungen vervielfältigt und ein wenig Nachforschung in Plattengeschäften oder Bibliotheken wird sie sicherlich ans Licht bringen. Bei Schwierigkeiten wenden Sie sich an ein Spezialgeschäft für Jazzmusik, wie z.B. "Ray's Jazz Shop" oder "Mole Jazz" in London.

Begleitung

Die Akkordfolgen der meisten Jazzmelodien, einschließlich der des Parkerschen Repertoires, bestehen aus 5 oder 6 Akkordgrundtypen:

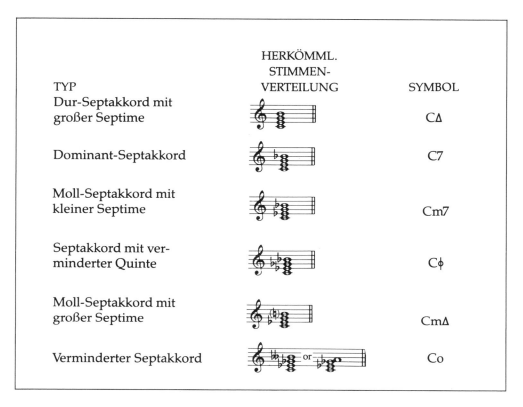

TYP	HERKÖMML. STIMMEN-VERTEILUNG	SYMBOL
Dur-Septakkord mit großer Septime		C∆
Dominant-Septakkord		C7
Moll-Septakkord mit kleiner Septime		Cm7
Septakkord mit verminderter Quinte		Cø
Moll-Septakkord mit großer Septime		Cm∆
Verminderter Septakkord	or	Co

Die einfachste wirkungsvolle Stimmenverteilung dieser Akkorde bei Klavier- oder Gitarrenbegleitung ist, nur den Grundton, die Terz und die Septime zu spielen, und die Quinte wegzulassen. Auf dem Klavier sollte der Grundton mit der linken Hand gespielt werden und die Terz und Quinte mit der rechten Hand. Bei dieser Stimmenverteilung dient der Moll-Septakkord mit kleiner Septime auch als Septakkord mit verminderter Quinte; dabei wird die Anzahl der Akkordtypen in der Liste auf fünf reduziert.

Dieses Verfahren wird "Stimmenverteilung mit möglichst wenig Tönen" genannt. Wenn wir dazu den Begriff der Stimmführung mit "möglichst wenig Bewegung" nehmen, kann eine II-V-I-Akkordfolge wie folgt gespielt werden:

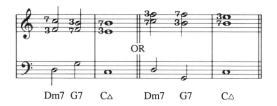

Dm7 G7 C∆   Dm7 G7 C∆

Diese Kombination von Stimmenverteilung und Stimmführung kann zusammengefaßt werden als das "Prinzip der möglichst wenig Töne und möglichst wenig Bewegung". Es kann bei fast allen Jazz-Akkordfolgen, einschließlich bei denen in dieser Sammlung, wirkungsvoll angewendet werden.

Um der Baßstimme willen sind erste und zweite Umkehrungen manchmal notwendig. Diese werden durch das Akkordsymbol über dem dazugehörenden Baßton bezeichnet:

$$\frac{F7}{A} \qquad \frac{F7}{C}$$
1. Umk. 2. Umk.

Die Stimmenverteilung der Akkorde in der Klavierstimme basiert auf dem Prinzip "möglichst wenig Töne, möglichst wenig Bewegung", aber die Akkorde sind manchmal durch eine oder mehrere Erweiterungen (None, Undezime und Tredezime), sowie an gegebener Stelle mit übermäßigen oder verminderten Quinten ergänzt. Die Art der Stimmenverteilung ist jener, die von Parkers bevorzugten Pianisten, Duke Jordan und Al Haig auf Originalaufnahmen zu hören ist, ähnlich, aber sie ist keine genaue Transkription dieser Aufnahmen. Russel hat Haigs Stil der Begleitung mit Akkorden ('comping') gut beschrieben: "Haig spielt nicht im Viervierteltakt oder in regelmäßigen Vierteln Klavier . . . Seine Akkorde sind gut gewählt und fein abgestuft, die Stimmen sind gut verteilt. Die Akkorde sind in das Gefüge der Rhythmusgruppe, deren Bestandteil er ist, eingebaut." (Aus: Ross Russell, *Bird Lives!*, Quarter Books 1973).

Akkordintervalle, die erhöht werden sollen, haben das +Zeichen davor (+ allein bedeutet eine übermäßige Quinte). Tönen, die erniedrigt werden sollen, ist das Zeichen ♭ vorangestellt. Das Symbol für die Dominante, gefolgt von "sus 4" bedeutet, daß die Terz durch einen Vorhaltston, die Quarte, ersetzt werden soll.

Die ausgeschriebenen Akkorde für Klavier sind im Viervierteltakt geschrieben, d.h. als Halbe Noten auf dem starken Taktteil, aber der Begleiter soll natürlich die rhythmische Stellung der Akkorde variieren, um einen authentischen "Comping"-Stil zu erreichen (wie obige Beschreibung des Stils von Haig empfiehlt).

Die Klavierstimme ist für die Themen bestimmt, doch normalerweise paßt sie auch zu den Soli. Manchmal (z.B. in *Ornithology*) gibt es kleine Unterschiede zwischen der Akkordfolge des Themas und der, die bei der Improvisation gespielt wird.

Klavierspieler, die diese Transkriptionen spielen wollen, werden eine Stimmenverteilung für die Begleitung mit der linken Hand vornehmen müssen. Eigentlich genügt eine Baßlinie aus Einzeltönen, die aus der Unterstimme der ausgeschriebenen Akkorde gebildet werden kann. Dazu kann man die Terz und die Septime (bzw. die Septime und die Terz) hinzufügen, um die Grundharmonie zu vervollständigen. Diejenigen, die die Stimmenverteilung der linken Hand mit Grundton, Septime und Terz, nicht spielen können, (d.h., die eine Dezime nicht greifen können), dürfen entweder den Grundton oder die Terz (Dezime) auslassen. (Weitere Informationen über die Stimmenverteilung der Akkorde siehe Lionel Grigson, *Practical Jazz*, Stainer & Bell 1988).

Diskographie der Transkriptionen

Aufnahmedaten und Ausführende in chronologischer Reihenfolge:

Moose the Mooche, Hollywood, 28. März 1946
Parker (Altsaxophon), Miles Davis (Trompete), Lucky Thompson (Tenorsaxophon), Dodo Marmarosa (Klavier), Arvin Garrison (Gitarre), Vic McMillan (Baß), Roy Porter (Schlagzeug)
Erhältlich auf *Bird Symbols*, Charlie Parker Records PLP-407 und *Charlie Parker on Dial*, Vol. 1, Spotlite Records 101

Scrapple from the Apple, New York, 4. November 1947
Parker, Davis, Duke Jordan (Klavier), Tommy Potter (Baß), Max Roach (Schlagzeug)
Erhältlich auf *Memorial Charlie Parker*, Vogue CLD.753 (eine andere Version findet sich auf *Bird Symbols*)

Au Privave, New York, 17. Januar 1951
Parker, Davis, Walter Bishop (Klavier), Teddy Kotick (Baß), Max Roach (Schlagzeug)
Erhältlich auf *Swedish Schnapps* (*The Genius of Charlie Parker* No.8) Verve V6-8010

Blues for Alice, New York, 8. August 1951
Parker, Red Rodney (Trompete), John Lewis (Klavier), Ray Brown (Baß), Kenny Clarke (Schlagzeug)
Auch auf *Swedish Schnapps*, s.o.

Confirmation, New York, 4. August 1953
Parker, Al Haig (Klavier), Percy Heath (Baß), Max Roach (Schlagzeug)
Erhältlich auf *Now's the Time* (*The Genius of Charlie Parker* No.3), Verve/Polydor 2304095 Mono

Ornithology, Boston, 22. September 1953
Parker, Red Garland (Klavier), Bernie Griggs (Baß), Roy Haynes (Schlagzeug)
Erhältlich auf *Charlie Parker at Storyville*, Blue Note BT 85108

Anmerkungen über die Themen und Soli

(Die hier als a), b), usw. bezeichneten Phrasen, sind dementsprechend in den Transkiptionen zu finden)

I. AU PRIVAVE (1951)
Form: 12takiger Blues

THEMA

Dieses optimistische, heitere Thema ist ein ziemlich typischer Parkerscher Blues-Kopf, zusammengefügt aus einer Reihe kurzer melodischer oder rhythmischer Motive, die eine fast ununterbrochene 12takige Phrase bilden. Die Takte 1-3 sind eine starke Behauptung der Tonika in der Dur-Tonart, wenn man den üblichen Subdominantakkord, der im zweiten Takt eines Blues vorkommt, nicht beachtet. Die Anfangsmotive der Parkerschen Blues-Köpfe sind oft von dieser Art; sie sind dem Dur-Dreiklang nahe und enthalten den Leitton öfter als die kleine Septime der Bluestonleiter. Die kleine Septime (E♭) wird, wie in einem alten Blues, bis zum vierten Takt aufgehoben, um die nachfolgende Subdominante anzukündigen.

Die am deutlichsten erkennbaren Bluesmotive in Parkers Bluesthemen, die die Töne der Bluestonleiter benutzen, werden manchmal für die Subdominantakkorde der Takte 5-6 aufgehoben, wie in *Au Privave* und *Blues for Alice*.

Beachten Sie die positive rhythmische Struktur jedes Motivs und die Verwendung der Synkope, um bestimmte Töne hervorzuheben. Die Takte 1 und 2 implizieren ein Gegenmetrum von 3+3+2 Schlägen zum Viervierteltakt. Die Figur in Takt 5 hat das gleiche Schema, 3+3+2, aber in Achtelnoten. Dies ist auch die wichtigste rhythmische Figur (Takt 1 usw.) von *Moose the Mooche*.

SOLO – Drei Chorusse, 36 Takte
ERSTER CHORUS

a) Diese Phrase sitzt auf den Takten 2 und 3, d.h. eher in der Mitte der ersten vier Takte als an deren Anfang. Die Subdominante wird wieder zugunsten einer klaren Behauptung der Tonika ignoriert. Die Melodie von Takt 2, 2. Schlag bis zu Takt 3, 2. Schlag ist eine genaue Transposition der ersten fünf Schläge des Themas von *Ornithology* – beginnt jedoch auf einem unbetonten statt auf einem betonten Taktteil. Die letzte Note der ganzen Phrase nimmt die erwartete kleine Septime von Takt 4 um 1½ Takte vorweg. Parker verwendet diese Vorwegnahme – die "frühe Septime" – auch in den Soli von *Blues for Alice* (1. Chorus, Takt 3) und *Confirmation* (1. Chorus, Takt 27).

b) Zwei kleine Motive, jedes mit einem aus vier Sechzehnteln bestehenden Auftakt, über der Subdominante in den Takten 5 und 6. Das zweite Motiv ist beinahe eine Wiederholung des ersten, aber mit D♭ statt D, wobei der Subdominant-Mollakkord angedeutet wird.

c) Diese fast 4½ Takte lange Phrase sitzt auf der Grenzlinie zwischen den zweiten vier Takten und letzten vier Takten des Chorus. Sie besteht aus zwei miteinander verbundenen "Annäherungsphrasen", die sich zuerst zur Subdominantparallele (Gm7, Takt 9) und dann ohne Pause bis Takt 11 fortsetzen.

Takt 7 ist das archetypische "Bop break", eine vom Leitton durch den Tonikadreiklang aufsteigende Figur aus einem Achtel und einer Triole, gefolgt von einem chromatischen Lauf abwärts vom Leitton (vgl. Break für Solo, der im Takt 31 des *Ornithology*-Themas beginnt).

Takt 8 veranschaulicht eine übliche Parkersche Annäherung an die Subdominantparallele (in dieser Tonart Gm7), um die vier letzten Takte eines Blues einzuleiten. Außer seiner letzten Note ist dieser Takt im Prinzip eine abwärts gespielte harmonische g-moll-Tonleiter über den Akkorden II7 und V7 (Aø und D7). (Eine andere Art der Annäherung an die Subdominantparallele findet sich in *Blues for Alice* Solo, 2. Chorus, Takt 8).

Eingebettet in Takt 9 (Töne 2-5) ist eine aus einem Achtel und einer Triole bestehende Figur derjeniger in Takt 7 ähnlich, aber transponiert, um von der None von Gm7 ihren Anfang zu nehmen. In den Takten 10 und 11 ist die Linie um eine aufsteigende Figur aufgebaut, die von der Quinte über die übermäßige Quinte der Dominante (C7) zur Terz der Tonart (F) führt.

ZWEITER CHORUS

d) Ein kurzes Motiv, das die Tonika stark und auf reizende Weise wieder bestätigt. Zur gleichen Zeit wird der Viervierteltakt durch deutliche Akkordtöne (Grundton und Quinte) betont, die auf den ersten und dritten Schlag von Takt 1 gesetzt werden.

e) Eine lange gewundene 5taktige Phrase, die in Takt 2 mit einem Auftakt aus 3 Achteln anfängt und sich Takt 5 (Subdominante) mit einer allgemeinen Abwärtsbewegung nähert, sich über die Takte 5 und 6 fortsetzt und in Takt 7 zur Tonika zurückkehrt. Vom Auftakt bis Takt 4 stört die Auswahl der Töne in ihrem Verhältnis zu den Akkorden das Metrum in einer Weise, die nicht leicht zu analysieren ist. Beginnend beim vierten Schlag von Takt 2 scheinen sich die Töne in Dreivierteltakte zu ordnen. Die Linie wird auf B7 (Takt 5) aufgelöst und setzt sich dann fort mit einer kühn aufsteigenden Figur, die die erniedrigte None (H), die übermäßige Undezime (E) und die Tredezime (G) einschließt, bevor sie auf unkomplizierte Weise zur Tonika zurückkehrt.

f) Eine Pause von vier Schlägen geht dem aus vier Achteln bestehenden Auftakt zu einer Parker-Spezialität voran – dem "Korkenzieher" in doppelten Notenwerten über Gm7 und C7 nach F. Der "Korkenzieher"-Effekt hält über dem ersten Halbtakt von Gm7 (Takt 9) an:

Obgleich Parker diesen Kunstgriff oft anwendet, läßt er den Zuhörer immer in Unsicherheit über die Art der Fortführung des "Korkenziehers". In diesem Fall setz er die doppelten Notenwerte durch den ganzen Takt und den darauffolgenden Takt (C7) fort und verwendet dabei eine wirksame Chromatik (+5 und ♭9) in der zweiten Hälfte des Takts bevor er die Phrase auf der Quinte der Tonika in Takt 11 auflöst.

DRITTER CHORUS

g) Parker schmückt die zwei letzten Takte des zweiten Chorus mit zwei eleganten Floskeln, die ohne Pause zu einer nüchternen Bluesfigur in den Takten 1-3 führen – tatsächlich bis jetzt die erste Anwendung von Blues-tönen (verminderte Quinte und kleine Terz der Blues-tonleiter) in diesem Solo.

h) Ein aus drei Tönen bestehender Auftakt in Takt 4 führt von einer vorweggenommenen None auf F7 zu einer durch die Subdominante (B7) absteigenden Phrase, die auf dem letzten Schlag von Takt 5 auf wirkungsvolle Weise abgebrochen wird. Nach einer Pause von 2 Schlägen führt eine Triole (die die Moll-Sub-dominante implizieren) zur Tonika (Takt 7) zurück. Trotz der dazwischenliegenden Pause bilden die zwei Teile dieser Phrase eine gesamte Idee.

i) Noch eine Annäherungsphrase an die Subdominant-parallele (vgl. Takt 8 mit Takt 8 im ersten Chorus) die nach dem ersten Schlag von Takt 9 endet. Die ganze Phrase ist so konstruiert, daß sie klingt, als ob sie einen Schlag zu spät gekommen wäre. Wenn sie einen Schlag früher angefangen hätte, würde sie natürlich auf dem letzten Schlag von Takt 8 enden (mit dem letzten Achtel als eine Vorwegnahme des nächsten Abschlags).

j) Nach einer Pause von 1½ Schlägen führt ein aus drei Achteln bestehender Auftakt zur Dominante (C7) in Takt 10, auf dessen ersten Schlag Parker sowohl die erniedrigte als auch die erhöhte (übermäßige) None in einer Triolenwendung erklingen läßt. Diese Phrase setzt sich bis in Takt 11 hinein fort, wo sie auf dem drit-ten Schlag verspätet aufgelöst wird, nachdem sie einen eingefügten IV-moll-Akkord im ersten Halbtakt ange-deutet hat.

k) Eine einfache Phrase, die das Ende dieses Teils signalisiert, führt in den nachfolgenden Chorus hinein.

2. SCRAPPLE FROM THE APPLE (1947)

Form: AABA 32 Takte

Eine alternative Aufnahme dieser frühen Quintett-version. Die Akkordfolgen in den A-Teilen sind im wesentlichen diejenigen von Fats Wallers *Honeysuckle Rose* (eine Melodie, die Parker als Teenager aufnahm), während die Akkordfolgen des B-Teils (Mitte-8) die-jenigen des Mittelteils von *I Got Rhythm* (nach F transponiert) sind. Die Akkordfolgen von *Scrapple* sind daher eine Hybride zweier grundlegender AABA-Akkordfolgen.

THEMA

Die ersten vier Takte sind ein gutes Beispiel von Parkers Art, Phrasen über den Akkorden II7 und V7 in der Dur-tonart zu komponieren. Beachten Sie, wie in Takt 1 die große und kleine Septime (F♯ und F♮) zusammen mit II7 (Gm7) verwendet werden, und wie die kleine Sep-time nach einer abwärtsführenden Terz sich im nächsten Takt auf der Quinte der Dominante (C7), statt auf der üblichen Terz der Dominante, auflöst. Takt 3 endet mit einer vorweggenommenen und nicht auf-gelösten verminderten None von C7.

Wie die meisten Parkerschen Themen ist der *Scrapple*-Kopf stark rhythmisch und kann als Schlagzeugsolo gespielt werden.

Die Mitte-8 ist improvisiert. Die Phrase *a)* erstreckt sich über 2 Takte von A7 und einen Takt und einen Schlag von D7. Die kleine und große None erklingen auf dem zweiten Schlag von Takt 18. Das Cis am Anfang von Takt 19 scheint ein falscher Ton zu sein, "gehört" aber zu A7 des vorhergehenden Takts.

Phrase *b)* der Mitte ist eine kurze aber triumphierend aufsteigende Figur in doppelten Notenwerten nach G7, die ein hohes G erreicht, das auf wirkungsvolle Weise vom letzten Schlag von Takt 21 bis zum ersten Schlag des nächsten Takts gehalten wird, bevor sie abwärts zur Tredezime und None führt. Eine Pause von einem Schlag geht dem aus Sechzehnteln bestehenden Auf-takt zu Phrase *c)* voran, die ein weiteres Beispiel für den "Korkenzieher" in doppelten Notenwerten über Gm7 und C7 (Takte 23 und 24) ist. Vor der letzten Floskel ist eine Pause.

SOLO – ein Chorus (32 Takte)

ERSTE 8

d), *e)* und *f)* Die Erste 8 entfaltet eine Folge von drei Phrasen von zunehmender Länge und Komplexität. Die dritte und längste Phrase, *f)*, zeigt eine charakteristische Durchgangschromatik bevor sie zum Anfang der Zweiten 8 führt. Beachten Sie die schräge Verwendung von A♭m7 in der zweiten Hälfte von Takt 8, die durch ihre Septime und None (G♭ und D♭) zur Quinte (D) des folgenden Akkords (Gm7) führt. (Vgl. *Ornithology* Solo, 1. Chorus, Takt 14.)

ZWEITE 8

g) Phrase in doppelten Notenwerten von C7 zurück nach Gm7. (Für Parker ungewöhnlich, scheint sie etwas unruhig ausgeführt worden zu sein).

h) Eine ziemlich typische Parkersche Akkordfolge von der Dominante zur Tonika (Takte 12-13), die weiterhin vielmehr die zweiten vier Takte des Akkordwechsels von *I Got Rhythm*, als die übliche *Scrapple*-Akkordfolge andeutet, d.h. zur Subdominante im folgenden Takt (Takt 14) geht und dann in nächsten Takt zurückkehrt. Die wiederholte Wendung in den Takten 14 und 15 erweckt die Vorstellung von zwei Dreivierteltakten, die auf dem zweiten Schlag von Takt 14 beginnen (ein Kreuzmetrum von 1+3+3+1 anstelle von 4+4 Schlägen). Diesen Schluß könnte man die "Schlangenlinie" nennen.

MITTE-8

i) Die klassische Art, mit den ersten drei Takten der *Rhythm* − Mitte fertigzuwerden. Die ersten zwei Takte (17 und 18) sind wie die Annäherung einer Dominante zu einer Tonika im dritten Takt (19) − die sich jedoch zur Septime fortsetzen. (Vgl. diesen Takt mit *Blues for Alice*, 1. Chorus, Takt 3). Ihr Schluß gibt dieser optimistischen Phrase einen Hauch von Pathos. Wenn der darauf folgende G7-Akkord als die Subdominante von D7 betrachtet wird, dann hat die Endung der Phrase eine Bedeutung, die derjenigen der "frühen" Septime in Takt 3 eines Blues ähnlich ist.

j) Eine fein ausgedachte fünftaktige Phrase, die zum ersten Takt der Letzten 8 führt. Takt 21 erhält seine harmonische Brillianz durch die Verwendung der Tredezime und der None zusammen mit der hellen übermäßigen Undezime von G7.

LETZTE 8

k), l) und m) Ohne Takt 25 (den Schluß der vorhergehenden Phrase) mitzuzählen, schließt der Chorus mit zwei Phrasen von abnehmender Länge, eine Umkehrung des Verfahrens der Ersten 8.

3. MOOSE THE MOOCHE (1946)
Form: AABA 32 Takte (Rhythmuswechsel)

THEMA

Eine frühe Komposition über den Akkordfolgen von *I Got Rhythm*, die vielleicht Parkers am strengsten organisiertes Thema ist. *Moose* ist schwer, auswendig zu lernen, einerseits aufgrund der Unterschiede zwischen den Ersten und Zweiten Achten und andererseits, weil die Mitte-8 komponiert und nicht so sehr zur Improvisation offengelassen worden ist. (Die meisten "Rhythmusköpfe" haben fast identische Haupt-Achte, so daß man in Wirklichkeit nur 8 Takt auswendig lernen muß, weil die Mitte-8 improvisiert wird).

Das Hauptmotiv ist die rhythmische melodische Figur von Takt 1 − ein weiteres Beispiel der 3+3+2 −

Aufteilung des Takts − wie sie auch im Thema von *Au Privave* (Takt 5) vorkommt. Diese rhythmische Figur erscheint sowohl in den ersten und dritten Takten jeder Haupt-8 als auch in den Takten 15 und 31, d.h. insgesamt achtmal.

Das melodisch-harmonische Schema der ersten vier Takte der Hauptachten kann einfach auf I-V-I-V reduziert werden. In den letzten vier Takten wird das Schema von einer Melodie und einer Akkordfortschreitung gefolgt, die zur Subdominante und zurück führt. Aber die zweiten vier Takte der Zweiten 8 haben eine andere "zur Subdominante und zurück" Melodie und einen Schluß, der so konzipiert ist, daß er zur Mitte-8 mit einer vorweggenommenen None auf D7 führt.

Die Mitte-8 kontrastiert abgestoßene Synkopen (Takte 17, 20 und 24) mit fließenden Achteln (Takte 19, 21 und 22). Beachten Sie die Verwendung von Nonen und Tredezimen über den Akkorden D7 (Takt 18) und G7 (Takt 19) und den Gebrauch der großen und kleinen None über F7 (Takt 24).

SOLO − ein Chorus (32 Takte)

Im Kontrast zum gedrängten Stil des Themas besteht das Solo hauptsächlich aus längeren Phrasen mit mehr Pausen.

ERSTE 8

a) Eine Eröffnungsfigur, die um die Tonika herum aufgebaut ist.

b) Bei dieser Phrase, die auf demselben Taktteil wie die vorhergehende Phrase beginnt, jedoch einen halben Takt länger ist, handelt es sich um eine typische "zur Subdominante und zurück" (über IV moll) führende Phrase.

ZWEITE 8

c) Eine kurze von der Tonika zur Dominante führende Phrase, die nur die ersten zwei Takte in Anspruch nimmt.

d) Eine lange Phrase (fast 5 Takte), die sich über die zwei 4taktigen Abschnitte der Zweiten 8 erstreckt. Die Takte 11 und 12 nähern sich der Tonika mit einer allgemeinen Abwärtsbewegung. Nachdem die Phrase die Tonika in Takt 13 erreicht hat, setzt sie sich über Takt 14 (IV und IVm) fort und geht zurück zur Tonika in Takt 15.

Vergleichen Sie die Länge und Stellungen der Phrasen in diesen ersten zwei Achten. Die Erste 8 besteht aus einer Phrase je viertaktigem Abschnitt (Symmetrie). Einen Gegensatz dazu bildet die Zweite 8 mit einer kurzen Phrase, welche die ersten zwei Takte in Anspruch nimmt und von einer sich über die viertaktigen Abschnitte erstreckenden langen Phrase gefolgt wird (Asymmetrie).

MITTE-8

e) Nach einer aufsteigenden Figur, bestehend aus einem

Achtel und einer Triole (Quinte, None, Undezime und Tredezime), gewinnt der erste Akkord (D7) der Mitte-8 einen beliebten Parkerschen Effekt: eine absteigende Bewegung von einer Tredezime durch eine übermäßige Undezime zu einer None und Septime, mit einer Wiederholung der Tredezime und übermäßigen Undezime im nächsten Takt (18). Merken Sie, wie sich die Wirkung der übermäßigen Undezime im nächsten Akkord (G7, Takt 19) wiederholt, obgleich dies nicht durch eine exakte Transposition des ersten Motivs geschieht.

f) Diese Phrase nähert sich der Dominante (F7) über ihre Dominante (C7). Mit einem chromatischen Durchgangston (C♭) ist die Tonleiter von Anfang der Phrase bis zum vorletzten Ton von Takt 21 die melodische f-moll-Tonleiter, (die aufsteigende Form abwärts gespielt). Vergleichen Sie die Phrase, die in Takt 23 endet, mit dem *Scrapple*-Solo, Takt 19 und dem *Confirmation*-Solo, 2. Chorus, Takte 12 und 30.

LETZTE 8
g) Eine einfache fröhliche Phrase, die die Tonika wieder bestätigt.

h) Wie die zweite Phrase *(d))* der Zweiten 8 setzt sich diese Phrase über die Verbindungsstelle zwischen viertaktigen Abschnitten fort. Beachten Sie die chromatische Annäherung an Cm7 (Subdominantparallele, Takt 28) über Dm7 und D♭ m7 in Takt 27 und den Gebrauch einer einfachen B-Dur-Tonleiter über Cm7 und F7 in Takt 28.

i) Der Schluß, der über den letzten Takt in den darauffolgenden Chorus führt.

4. ORNITHOLOGY (1953)
Form: ABAC 32 Takte

THEMA
Die Akkordfolgen sind, mit der einen oder anderen Veränderung, die der neuen Melodie entsprechen, vom Lied *How High the Moon* abgeleitet. Der Trompeter Benny Harris, ein früher Kollege, hat wahrscheinlich bei der Komposition mitgewirkt.

Die früheste Version von *Ornithology* wurde im Jahre 1946 während derselben Session (für Dial Records) aufgenommen, die *Moose the Mooche* und die historische *Night in Tunisia* hervorbrachte. In späteren Versionen verzichtete Parker auf die vom ganzen Orchester gespielten Triolenschlußfiguren zu den 16taktigen Abschnitten der Originalmelodie, die einer Besetzung mit drei Hörnern entsprachen, zugunsten von Schlußfiguren, die für ein oder zwei Hörner geeigneter waren.

Die Akkordfolgen beginnen mit zwei Takten in der Tonika (G); danach modulieren sie zuerst nach F über Gm7 und C7 und dann mit der gleichen Akkordfolge (II7 und V7 der neuen Tonart) nach E♭ . Aus der Durtonleiter wird eine Molltonleiter, die dann als der erste, die Dominante vorbereitende Schritt des Tonartwechsels, enthüllt wird.

Dementsprechend gestaltet Parker zuerst eine kühne Dur-Phrase (Takt 1 bis zum 1. Schlag von Takt 2), dann wiederholt er ihren Anfang in der Moll-Tonart, bevor er die wahre Bedeutung dieser Phrase (wie das hohe F sie zeigt) als den Vorboten von F-Dur enthüllt. Diese Tonart wird dann in die Molltonart verwandelt, um nach E♭ in Takt 9 über B7 zu führen. (Um der Melodie zu entsprechen, sollte hier Akkord E♭ 7 anstelle von E♭ Δ benutzt werden, obgleich letzterer wahrscheinlich für eine Improvisation geeigneter wäre.)

Nach E♭ führen die Akkordfolgen zur Mollvariante der Tonika über ihre II7 und V7-Akkorde (Aϕ und D7) zurück. Die vier letzten Takte der Zweiten 8 sind eine zur Dritten 8 führende Wendung von doppelter Länge (je Takt Hm7, E7, Am7 und D7). Die Dritte 8 ist eine Wiederholung der Ersten 8, und die Letzte 8 verkürzt die Wendung auf zwei Takte, um in den zwei letzten Takten die Tonika zu erreichen. Parker nutzt diese Takte für einen zu seinem ersten Solo-Chorus führenden kurzen Break. (Vgl. Takt 1 dieses Breaks (Takt 31) mit Takt 7, 1. Chorus, *Au Privave*-Solo). Beachten Sie die wirkungsvolle übermäßige Quinte auf der implizierten Dominante D7 im zweiten Takt dieses Breaks.

SOLO – drei Chorusse, 96 Takte
In dieser Liveaufnahme, die während einer Session in einem Bostoner Klub aufgenommen wurde, umspannt Parkers Ideenreichtum drei ganze Chorusse. Keine Phrase-für-Phrase Analyse wird hier gemacht, teilweise wegen der Länge des Solos, aber auch weil die wesentlichen Merkmale von Parkers Stil in dieser Sammlung genügend beschrieben worden sind, um ein Verständnis dieses prachtvollen Solos ohne weitere Erläuterungen zu ermöglichen.

Trotzdem seien hier einige Glanzpunkte erwähnt:

1. Die Takte 3 und 4 des ersten Chorus veranschaulichen die Interpretation einer 2taktigen II-V-Akkordfolge, wobei Gm7 nach C7 zu Gm GmΔ | Gm7 C7 wird und dabei einen Aufbau der Phrase um die absteigende Linie aus halben Noten G-F♯ -F♮ -E ermöglicht.

2. Die Phrase *n)* ist ein unerwartetes rhythmisch freies Zitat der ersten Phrase des Liedes *Tenderly* (Original im Dreivierteltakt).

3. Der Höhepunkt des Solos kurz nach der ersten Hälfte ist die Dritte 8 des zweiten Chorus. Dieser wird in den Takten 16 und 17 (über den Schluß der Zweiten 8 hinweg) durch einen herabsteigenden Lauf von F angekündigt (Phrase *o)*). Die Phrase *p)* (Takt 18) ist eine Finte über der Tonika in doppelten Notenwerten – dann spielt Parker los mit einem rasenden und verschlung-

enen "Korkenzieher" in doppelten Notenwerten (Phrase q)), der sich über Gm7 und C7 bis zu einem ganzen Takt in F-Dur erstreckt, um mit einer Phrase, die fast eine Transposition der ersten Phrase des Themas ist, zu schließen.

4. Gegen Ende des Solos gibt es eine bemerkenswerte 9taktige Phrase, (z)), von auffallender Kontinuität, die zuerst ein scheinbares Zitat entwickelt und dann zu einer weiteren transponierten Erwähnung des Themenanfangs in Takt 25 (E♭) führt.

5. BLUES FOR ALICE (1951)
Form: 12taktiger Blues ("Round the Clock")

THEMA
Das unkomplizierte *Au Privave* war Parkers Neujahrs-Blues für das Jahr 1951 (aufgenommen am 17. Januar). Das kontrastierende *Blues for Alice* wurde acht Monate später aufgenommen, und ist auf die Variation der Bluesfolgen aufgebaut, die als "Bird Blues", "Swedish Blues" oder in Großbritannien "Round the Clock" Blues bekannt sind.

Nachfolgend die einfachste Darstellung der "Alice"-Akkordfolgen, verglichen mit den grundlegenden Akkordfolgen des "Modern" Blues.

GRUNDLEGENDE AKKORDFOLGE

F	B7	F	F7	
B7	B7	F	D7	
Gm7	C7	F D7	Gm7 C7 ||

ALICE-AKKORDFOLGE

F	A7	Dm	F7	
B	Bm	F	A♭o	
Gm7	C7	F D7	Gm7 C7 ||

Die Hauptunterschiede liegen in den ersten acht Takten. In den ersten vier Takten führen die *Alice*-Akkordfolgen zur Mollvariante in Takt 3. In den zweiten vier Takten verläuft die Rückkehr zur Tonika über IVm und die Subdominantparallele wird über den verminderten Akkord auf ♭III erreicht.

In schematisierter Form (die strenge Akkordfolge von "Round the Clock") lauten die Akkordfolgen von *Alice* wie folgt:

F△	Em7 / Eø	A7	Dm7 G7	Cm7 F7	
B△	Bm7	E♭7	Am7 D7	A♭m7 D♭7	
Gm7	C7		F△ D7	Gm7 C7 ||

Während das "Round the Clock" Schema eine geeignete Begleitung zum Thema und Solo bildet, können diese genauso gut von den oben angegebenen einfacheren Akkordfolgen begleitet werden. (John Lewis, Klavier, ist diesen manchmal näher.) Mit anderen Worten, Parker verläßt sich nicht auf durchgehende Akkorde und kann eine Sequenz bis auf ihre wesentlichen Akkordfolgen vereinfachen.

Die von den *Alice*-Akkordfolgen gebotene kniffligste Modulation ist die durch die Akkorde A♭m7-D♭7 (oder durch jeden einzelnen Akkord) angedeutete (aber nicht vollzogene) Modulation in Takt 8 nach G♭-Dur. Beachten Sie die Melodie an dieser Stelle des Themas und auch die Phrase an der gleichen Stelle im zweiten Chorus des Solos – beide sind einen Halbton höher transponierte Varianten der ersten Phrase von *Honeysuckle Rose*.

Größtenteils fließt das Thema durch die Akkordfolgen und ist nicht bluesähnlich. Jedoch sind die letzten vier Töne von Takt 4 und der ganze Takt 5 eine tiefempfundene Bluesphrase (vgl. Takt 5 von *Au Privave*).

SOLO – drei Chorusse, 36 Takte
ERSTER CHORUS
a) Takt 1 betont die große Septime der Tonika auf dem ersten und dritten Schlag (Dissonanz auf dem starken Taktteil); Takt 2 scheint auf die Mollvariante auf einfache Weise zuzugehen. Aber in Takt 3 vermeidet Parker die erwartete Auflösung und nimmt statt dessen die Akkorde des folgenden Taktes vorweg – ein weiteres Beispiel der "frühen Septime".

b) Eine tief empfundene Bluesphrase über IV und IVm (Takte 5 und 6), die in Takt 7 zurück zur Tonika (oder III7) führt. Die letzten drei Töne dieses Takts sind die gleichen wie in Takt 3, aber diesmal haben sie eine andere Bedeutung – das letzte E♭ läßt die Akkorde in Takt 8 vorausahnen.

c) Eine kurze Phrase auf der Subdominantparallele.

d) Eine weitere Variation des "Korkenziehers" in doppelten Notenwerten, die diesmal nicht über II7 sondern vielmehr über dem Akkord V7 beginnt.

ZWEITER CHORUS
e) Eine Variation oder Entwicklung der Anfangsphrase *a)* des ersten Chorus, diesmal bis Takt 4 erweitert. In den Takten 3 und 4 sind zwei Motive die, je mit einem Doppelschlag anfangend, zuerst d-Moll und dann, nach kunstvoller Veränderung, F7 andeuten. Sie sind so gesetzt, daß die zwei Takte in 3+3+2 Schläge aufgeteilt werden.

f) Wie im vorhergehenden Chorus beginnt diese Phrase als eine Bluesphrase über IV und IVm. Sie wird dann erweitert und endet mit einer bekannten Idee, die kunstvoll transponiert wurde, um sich den Akkorden von Takt 8 anzupassen.

g) Doppelte Notenwerte über II-V-I. Diese Phrase scheint mit einem absichtlichen Fehlstart zu beginnen, als ob Parker möchte, daß der Zuhörer noch einen "Korkenzieher" erwartet, bricht aber dann ab, um sich auf andere Weise fortzusetzen.

DRITTER CHORUS

h) Ein über den letzten Takt des vorhergehenden Chorus ausdrucksvoll gehaltener Ton führt zu einer kurzen Figur auf der Tonika in Takt 1.

i) Diese Phrase führt zur Mollvariante und dann zu einem Septakkord auf der Tonika. Vergleichen Sie Takt 2 mit Takt 2 in den ersten beiden Chorussen. Jeder Takt hat ähnliche "Zutaten" (eigentlich eine harmonische d-Moll-Tonleiter), die jedoch jedesmal anders behandelt wird.

j) und k) werden als Einzelphrasen bezeichnet, die durch eine 1½taktige Pause getrennt sind. Zusammen betrachtet werden sie, wie in den beiden ersten Chorussen, wie IV und IVm einer Bluestonleiter behandelt.

l) II-V-I in doppelten Notenwerten wie im zweiten Chorus und wieder mit einem "absichtlichen Fehlstart", (aber mit anderen Tönen).

m) Der Ton wird bis zum darauffolgenden Takt gehalten. Eine Phrase in doppelten Notenwerten führt zum nachfolgenden Chorus.

ZUSAMMENFASSUNG

Insgesamt scheint dieses Stück eines von Parkers am sorgfältigsten komponierte Bluesimprovisation zu sein. Jeder Chorus ist in 4taktigen Abschnitten konstruiert, wobei die ersten vier Takte den Wechsel zur Mollvariante verdeutlichen. Die zweiten vier Takte stellen eine Bluesfigur über der Subdominante, und die vier letzten Takte eine Rückkehr zur Tonika in doppelten Notenwerten dar. Die Ähnlichkeit der Abschnitte verleiht dem ganzen Solo eine Gesamteinheit, die jedoch durch einen Reichtum an detaillierten Variationen zwischen den entsprechenden Abschnitten in jedem Chorus ausgeglichen wird.

6. CONFIRMATION (1953)
Form: AABA, 32 Takte

THEMA

Die Akkordfolgen in den ersten vier Takten der Haupt-Achte sind die gleichen wie in den ersten vier Takten von Blues for Alice, d.h. im wesentlichen F–A7–Dm7–F7.

Deswegen ist es interessant, die zwei Themen und Parkers Improvisationen in diesen Abschnitten zu vergleichen. Die Akkordfolgen von Confirmation setzen sich, wie ein abgekürzter Blues, mit einem Takt der Subdominante fort. Sie führen dann zu einem Halbschluß in der Ersten 8 und zu einem Ganzschluß in den Zweiten und Letzten Achten. Die Mitte-8 enthält zwei Modulationen, zuerst zur Subdominante (B) und danach zur erniedrigten Untermediante (Db) (= erniedrigte Mediante der Subdominante), wobei jede neue Tonart über ihre II-V erreicht wird. Der achte Takt besteht aus der Folge II-V, die nach F zurückführt.

Über den ähnlichen Akkordfolgen der Haupt-Achte (Zweite und Letzte 8 sind identisch, Zweite 8 identisch mit Ausnahme der letzten Takte), hat Parker ein hauptsächlich durchkomponiertes Thema mit wenig Wiederholungen ausgearbeitet. Die einzigen identischen Takte in den Haupt-Achten sind die Takte 2 und 26 und 4-5 und 28-9. Dies ist von einem einfachen AADA-Kopf wie Scrapple from the Apple, der wirklich nur aus acht Takten besteht, sehr weit entfernt. Dennoch vereinheitlicht Parker das Thema indem er Takte komponiert, die zum Teil einander ähneln (vgl. die Takte 1 und 25, letzte Schläge) und teilweise fast Umkehrungen voneinander sind (vgl. Takte 5 und 13). Die einfachste Methode, eine Einheit zu schaffen, sieht man in der Art, wie die ersten Phrasen von jeder Haupt-8 mit den gleichen drei synkopierten Tönen enden (obgleich sie verschieden beginnen).

Die ersten zwei Takte der Mitte-8 gründen auf dem Prinzip, je einen Takt von Cm7 und F7 in Halbtakte von Cm–CmΔ–Cm7–F7 aufzuteilen, um die abwärts führende Linie aus Halben C–H–B–A zu ermöglichen. Die Melodie folgt dieser Kontur, erniedrigt jedoch das erwartete A auf dem dritten Schlag von Takt 18 nicht zu einer Terz von F7, sondern zu einer übermäßigen None. (Vgl. Ornithology Solo, 1. Chorus, Takte 3-4).

Beachten Sie die komplizierte fallende Linie in Takt 21 (Eb m7). Takt 23 (Db Δ) ist die mit doppelten Notenwerten gespielte letzte Phrase der Dizzy Gillespie-Komposition Woody 'n' You.

SOLO – zwei Chorusse, 64 Takte

Aus den gleichen Gründen, aus denen keine Analyse des Ornithology Solos vorgenommen wurde, wird auch hier keine durchgeführt. Diese beiden Soli sind Meisterstücke, die Parker auf dem Höhepunkt seiner Schaffenskraft zeigen.

Ausgewählte Phrasen

A. PHRASEN MIT DOPPELTEN NOTENWERTEN

1. KORKENZIEHER

i) *Scrapple* (1947), Mitte, Phrase *c)*, Takte 23 und 24

ii) *Au Privave* (1951), 2. Chorus, Phrase *f)*, Takte 9-11

iii) *Blues for Alice* (1951), 1. Chorus, Phrase *d)*, Takte 10-11

iv) *Ornithology* (1953), 2. Chorus, Dritte 8, Phrase *q)*, Takte 19-22

2. ANDERE PHRASEN IN DOPPELTEN NOTENWERTEN

i) *Scrapple*, 1. Chorus, Mitte-8, Phrase *b)*, Takte 21 und 22

Solo, Zweite 8, Phrase *g)*, Takte 10 und 11

ii) *Blues for Alice*, 2. Chorus, Phrase *g)*, Takte 9-11 (der Fehlstart)

Dritter Chorus, Phrasen *l)* und *m)*, Takte 9-11

iii) *Ornithology*, 1. Chorus, Dritte 8, Phrase *g)*, Takte 20-22

iv) *Confirmation*, 1. Chorus, Zweite 8, Phrase *d)*, Takte 10-12

B. ERWEITERUNG UND ALTERATION DER DOMINANTE

i)   Übermäßige Quinte, steigend

Au Privave, 1. Chorus

ii) Übermäßige Quinte, fallend

Au Privave, 2. Chorus

iii) Erniedrigte None und erhöhte None

Au Privave, 3. Chorus

iv) Übermäßige Undezime (mit Tredezime und None)

Scrapple, Mitte-8

Moose the Mooche, Mitte-8

v) Alterierte Dominante (+9, ♭9, +5)

Ornithology, 2. Chorus

34

C. BLUESPHRASEN

Au Privave, 3. Chorus

Ornithology, 3. Chorus, Erste 8

Blues for Alice, 1. Chorus

Confirmation, letzter Chorus

D. SKALENARTIGE PASSAGEN

Harmonisches Moll (Gm)

Au Privave, 1. Chorus

Dur (B)

Moose the Mooche, Letze 8

Dur (F)

Ornithology, Thema, Takt 3

'Harmonisches Dur' (F)

Blues for Alice, 2. Chorus, Takt 10

E. AKKORDBRECHUNG

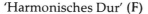

Moose the Mooche, Mitte-8, Takt 17

Ornithology, 1. Chorus

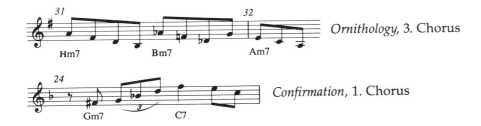

Ornithology, 3. Chorus

Confirmation, 1. Chorus

F. RHYTHMISCHE/METRISCHE KUNSTGRIFFE

1. SYNKOPE

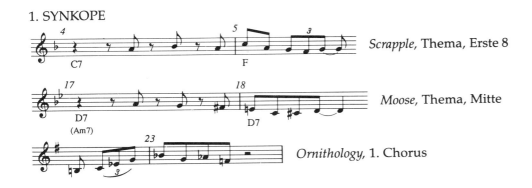

Scrapple, Thema, Erste 8

Moose, Thema, Mitte

Ornithology, 1. Chorus

2. GEGENMETRUM

Au Privave, Thema

Avant-Propos

La position centrale de Charlie Parker dans le développement du jazz est bien connue, mais de nombreuses difficultés apparaissent pour l'étudiant quand il s'agit de trouver un moyen d'entrer dans le style. En présentant un échantillon assez vaste des thèmes et des improvisations de Parker, accompagné d'une analyse par rapport à la fondation harmonique, on espère que cet album d'étude résoudra quelques-unes de ces difficultés.

Des transcriptions des solos sont devenues un moyen établi d'étudier le jazz. Pourtant, le résultat voulu – de s'améliorer en sa propre improvisation – ne peut pas se réaliser tout simplement en déchiffrant. Il faut comprendre pourquoi les notes et les phrases d'une transcription étaient tout d'abord choisies. La meilleure utilisation de cette sélection de Parker se fera en considérant les relations entre les solos et les séquences d'accords sur lesquelles ils sont basés.

Les six morceaux de cet album ont été choisis parmi la trentaine de copyrights de Parker disponibles au rédacteur. La selection est destinée à illustrer les formes principales dans lesquelles composait et improvisait Parker: le blues de 12 mesures, et la forme de la chanson de base de 32 mesures.

La séquence d'accords dans *Au Privave* représente le blues normal du jazz moderne (bebop). *Moose the Mooche* et *Scrapple from the Apple* sont basés sur des variantes étroitement liées de la forme AABA de 32 mesures (dont les sections A de 8 mesures sont harmoniquement presque identiques, tandis que B est une section en contraste; le 'middle 8').

Ornithology est basé sur une autre variante assez commune de la forme de 32 mesures, la structure de ABAC.

La séquence d'accords pour *Blues for Alice* est une variation beaucoup utilisée du blues moderne normal (*Au Privave* par exemple). Les quatre premières mesures de la séquence d'*Alice* se retrouvent dans *Confirmation* qui est encore un exemple de la forme AABA de 32 mesures.

Bref, le répertoire fondamental du jazz developpé par le bebop est vraiment composé des variantes d'un nombre limité de formes prototypiques. Si le débutant n'oublie pas ce fait, le travail essentiel de *mémoriser* un grand répertoire devrait devenir moins intimidant. L'étudiant qui apprend les six thèmes et les séquences d'accords de cette collection par coeur sera bien préparé à cette tâche.

LIONEL GRIGSON

Biographie en bref

Charlie Parker est né le 29 août 1920 à Kansas City. Son père, Charles Parker Sr., s'en est allé vers la fin des années 1920: dès lors Charles Parker est élevé par sa mère, Addie, toute seule, qui travaillait comme femme de ménage, et qui louait des chambres pour subvenir à ses propres besoins comme à ceux de son fils.

À l'âge de 13 ans, Parker montrait de l'intérêt pour les interprétations, entendues à la radio, de Rudy Vallee, un saxophoniste populaire, et sa mère lui a acheté un saxophone alto d'occasion à $45. L'instrument n'était qu'à peine jouable, et son intérêt s'est vite calmé. Mais à l'âge de 15 ans il est devenu membre de l'orchestre du lycée de Lincoln, d'abord en jouant du cor alto puis du cor baryton, sous la direction d'Alonzo Lewis, chef d'orchestre éminent. Il est devenu ami des élèves de Lewis plus âgés, y compris le pianiste Lawrence Keyes, et il a recommencé à faire du saxophone alto pour s'enrôler dans l'orchestre de Keyes, the Deans of Swing.

Parker s'intéressait alors d'une manière obsédante à la musique, mais sans grand résultat au début. Il a souffert d'une humiliation célèbre quand il a essayé de prendre part à une séance de jazz improvisé, avec le batteur de Count Basie, Jo Jones, en tête. Jones a marqué sa désapprobation aux efforts de Parker en jetant sa cymbale par terre. En 1937 Parker a joué avec l'orchestre du vocaliste George Lee pendant une saison d'été. Le pianiste, Carrie Lee, et le guitariste, Efferge Ware, lui apprenaient des accords et les relations des tonalités.

Le developpement musical de Parker était alors rapide. Deux influences importantes étaient le saxophoniste alto, Buster Smith, et Lester Young, la vedette du saxophone ténor de l'orchestre de Count Basie. Parker achetait les disques qu'avait fait Young avec Basie, les ralentissait à mi-vitesse sur un tourne-disque remontable, et mémorisait les solos de Young, note par note.

Dès cette époque environ, Parker était devenu

héroïnomane invétéré. Peut-être savait-il que sa dépendance se montrerait fatale, ce qui le poussait à s'appliquer résolument à la musique avec intensité. Une tragédie Faustienne était en train de naître.

En 1938 il est allé à Chicago puis à New York. Là, il faisait la vaisselle dans un restaurant où le pianiste résidant était Art Tatum, le musicien de jazz techniquement et harmoniquement le plus avancé de l'époque. Dans des séances d'improvisation avec le guitariste, Biddy Fleet, Parker travaillait des prolongations d'accords; il est arrivé à une découverte capitale en apprenant comment les intégrer dans ses lignes mélodiques. Il est retourné alors à Kansas City pour l'enterrement de son père, et est devenu ensuite membre de l'orchestre de Harlan Leonard pendant un temps très court.

En 1939 Parker est devenu membre d'un ensemble excellent de Kansas City, l'orchestre de Jay McShann, avec lequel il devait travailler plus ou moins régulièrement pendant les trois ans et demi suivants.

En 1941 Parker est retourné à New York avec l'orchestre de McShann. Avec d'autres musiciens animés des mêmes sentiments - Dizzy Gillespie (trompette), Thelonious Monk (piano), Kenny Clark (batterie) - il a consolidé ses expériences musicales dans des séances d'improvisations à Minton's Playouse. De ces séances naît un style révolutionnaire de jazz qu'on a appelé le bebop.

Il continue de travailler avec de grands orchestres (Earl Hines, Billy Eckstine); en 1944 il a formé un quintette avec Dizzy Gillespie pour être résidant au Three Deuces Club dans la 52ᵐᵉ rue de New York. Celui-ci était le premier groupe regulier de bebop.

Au mois de décembre 1945, avec Gillespie, Parker est allé à Hollywood pour un engagement de deux mois au club de Billy Berg. Il est resté en Californie en 1946, où il a enregistré des séances historiques pour Dial Records, puis il a souffert d'une depression, et il était hospitalisé pendant six mois.

La santé recouverte pendant un certain temps, Parker est retourné a New York en avril 1947 pour former un quintette avec le trompettiste Miles Davis (avec qui il avait fait des enregistrements en Californie). Il était à ce moment célèbre et le chef reconnu du nouveau mouvement de jazz. Les quelques années suivantes constituaient une période de succès croissant et de reconnaissance internationale. Pourtant, il était en sursis: son hospitalisation en Californie n'ayant apporté qu'un répit temporaire à sa dépendance.

En 1949 Parker a joué au Festival International de Jazz à Paris. En revenant à New York il a reformé son quintette avec Red Rodney (trompette). Un nouveau club, le Birdland, s'est ouvert en son honneur. Il a gagné le sommet de son succès commercial en 1951, en travaillant régulièrement avec son quintette et aussi avec un orchestre à cordes. Il s'était alors installé avec sa quatrième femme, Chan Parker, avec qui il a eu deux enfants.

Cependant, les efforts de Parker pour subvenir aux besoins de sa famille étaient gênés par la perte de sa carte de cabaret, ce qui voulait dire qu'il ne pouvait plus trouver du travail dans les clubs de New York. Bien qu'elle lui fût finalement rendue, le début des années 1950 n'étaient qu'un plateau provisoire. En 1954, déprimé par la mort de sa fille atteinte d'une pneumonie, et assailli par d'autres problèmes, Parker a tenté de se suicider et était de nouveau hospitalisé. Après cela son état s'est amelioré pendant un certain temps, mais dès 1955 Parker rechutait: il est mort, âgé de 34 ans dans l'apartement de la baronne Nica de Koenigswater à New York, le 12 mars 1955.

Le Style de Charlie Parker

'D'un point de vue intellectuel, le bebop était fascinant et sensationnel, et Charlie Parker en était le plus intellectuel de tous. La musique avait beaucoup d'esprit. L'intensité, la sensibilité de la musique était absolument fabuleux.' (Red Rodney)*

'L'aspect le plus complexe de bebop réside dans l'ingenuosité avec laquelle se créait la ligne melodique... Elle est composée d'un grand nombre de phrases, précisément calculées, dont chacune est une idée en soi-même qui peut être utilisée conjointement avec n'importe quelle autre phrase et sur n'importe quel air dont la structure des accords est chromatique ou diatonique. Cela peut se comparer à un puzzle qu'on peut assembler d'une centaine de façons differentes...' (Lennie Tristano)**

Red Rodney (trompettiste dans le dernier quintette avec lequel Parker jouait regulièrement) met le doigt sur la combinaison de l'esprit et de l'intellect qui est l'essentiel du style de Parker. Les remarques de

* d'après Ira Gitler, *Swing to Bop* (OUP 1985)

** d'après Robert George Reisner, *Bird*: The Legend of Charlie Parker (Citadel Press 1962)

Tristano (le professeur le plus important de jazz pendant les années 1940) constituent une analyse pénétrante de la méthode d'improvisation de Parker.

La base de la musique de Parker c'est le blues, ce qu'il a absorbé du milieu musical riche de Kansas City pendant la prohibition des années 1930. Un des premiers patrons de Parker, Jay McShann (qui était lui-même un pianiste redoutable de blues) le considérait comme un des plus grands exécutants du blues. Quelques exemples des phrasés purement blues dans ces transcriptions se trouvent dans les solos de *Au Privave*, premier refrain, mesures 4-7, et troisième refrain, mesures 1-3; et les solos de *Blues for Alice*, premier refrain, mesures 4-7, et troisième refrain, mesures 5-7.

Beaucoup des idées de Parker sont basées sur des cadences, des progressions des accords II 7 et V 7 à l'accord I (par exemple, en Do: Re mineur 7, Sol 7, Do △). Bien sûr, de telles progressions existaient déjà, mais Parker semble être le premier instrumentiste à vent à les utiliser systématiquement dans l'improvisation. Deux airs des années 1920 doivent être à l'origine de ces pensées du Parker adolescent: *Honeysuckle Rose* de Fats Waller, et (enregistré aussi par Waller), *Tea for Two*. On dit que celui-là est le premier air à avoir été mémorisé par Parker.

La première phrase de *Honeysuckle Rose* est harmonisée par la progression II-V:

Le motif d'*Honeysuckle*

On peut imaginer le jeune Parker qui travaillait des solos sur ce morceau en commençant par cette phrase (ou la première phrase de *Tea for Two*) et se posant la question "comment puis-je changer cette phrase, et où puis-je continuer?"

Parker se sert assez souvent des variations et des transpositions du motif de *Honeysuckle* alors que jamais le contexte d'une séquence d'accords ne le permet. Voir le solo de *Scrapple*, mesure 25; le thème de *Blues for Alice*, mesure 8, et aussi le solo, deuxième refrain, mesure 8.

Ensemble avec son emploi des progressions d'accords II-V ou II-V-I il y a cette technique fort travaillé de Parker de transposer des idées basées sur ces progressions (et sur des accords individuels) à n'importe quelle tonalité, et par conséquent, sa capacité de moduler en n'importe quelle tonalité qui se présente au cours d'un air. Jusqu'alors, aucun

musicien de jazz, à l'exception de Art Tatum, n'avait l'habilité de Parker de jouer des progressions harmoniques exigeantes. Le véhicule de travail pour ces techniques était un autre air préféré, *Cherokee* de Ray Noble, avec sa section centrale des modulations II-V-I descendantes (et son tempo épuisant):

La section centrale de Cherokee:

(Ton de Si♭)

D♭ m7 | G♭ 7| B△ | B△ | Bm7 | E7 | A△ | A△ |
Am7 | D7 | G△ | G△ | Gm7 | C7 | Cm7 | F7+ ‖

(jusqu'aux 16 dernières mesures)

À part son utilisation des cadences et des modulations, le trait original dans les lignes mélodiques de Parker réside en sa façon pleine d'imagination d'employer des extensions et d'autres 'tons colorés' pour ajouter aux tons de base de la fondamentale, 3ᶜᵉ, 5ᵗᵉ et 7ᵐᵉ de l'accord, en particulier au-dessus des accords du type de la 7ᵐᵉ de dominante.

Les extensions 'normales' d'un accord de 7ᵐᵉ de dominante sont la 9ᵐᵉ, 11ᵐᵉ et la 13ᵐᵉ qu'on obtient en étendant l'accord vers le haut à travers la gamme majeure dont il est la dominante:

Sol 7 comme V de Do majeur

Parker aimait beaucoup l'effet de la 11ᵐᵉ augmentée (+11) sur des accords de la dominante. Cette extension est le résultat de considérer un accord de 7ᵐᵉ de dominante comme un accord IV 7 d'une gamme mineure mélodique ascendante:

Sol 7 comme IV 7 de Re mineur mélodique (ascendant)

Pour avoir un exemple de l'emploi de Parker de la 11ᵐᵉ augmentée, voir le solo de *Moose the Mooche*, mesures 17-19 (les trois premières mesures de la section centrale).

Deux autres moyens d'obtenir des combinaisons intéressantes des 'tons colorés' sur l'harmonie de dominante se trouvent en plaçant l'accord soit dans une gamme diminuée, soit sur la note sensible d'une gamme mineure mélodique ascendante.

Sol 7 comme I d'une gamme diminuée (alternances des tons et des demi-tons)

Sol 7 (les bémols) sur la note sensible de La ♭ mineur mélodique (ascendant)

Ces deux gammes apportent à Sol 7 deux 9mes altérées - l'une bémol et l'autre dièse (♭9 et +9). Parker place souvent toutes deux de ces 9mes dans le doublé d'un triolet ou d'une croche et deux doubles-croches autour de la dominante (voir le solo de *Au Privave*, dernier refrain, mesure 10).

La gamme diminuée apporte aussi une 13me normale et une 11me augmentée (+11).

Dans la gamme mélodique de La ♭ mineur (ascendante) Sol 7 possède, à part les deux 9mes altérées (bémol et dièse), deux 5tes altérées, bémolisée et augmentée (♭5 et 5+). (On peut aussi considérer le + comme une 13me bémolisée). La 3ce majeure de Sol 7 (Si) est l'équivalent enharmonique de la 3ce mineure (Do ♭) de La ♭ mineur.

Une autre façon de représenter les relations entre l'accord de dominante et les combinaisons diverses des notes supplémentaires est d'ajouter ces dernières au tons de l'accord de base pour créer une gamme imaginaire de sa fondamentale (ce qui est à la base de beaucoup de l'enseignement de jazz aux États Unis et ailleurs - de George Russell et J. Aebersold, par exemple).

Les gammes qui en résultent sont des modes des gammes diatoniques dans lesquelles l'accord peut se situer diatoniquement.

Alors, pour Sol 7 comme V 7 de Do majeur nous obtenons:

Le mode mixolydien

Pour Sol 7 comme IV 7 de Re mineur mélodique (ascendant):

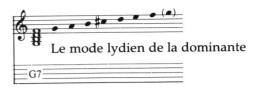

Le mode lydien de la dominante

(On appelle des fois celle-ci la gamme 'Lydienne de la Dominante'. Elle est le quatrième mode de la gamme mineur mélodique ascendante).

Pour Sol 7+, ou ♭ 5, sur la note sensible de La ♭ mineur mélodique (ascendant):

La gamme altérée de la dominante

(On appelle des fois celle-ci la gamme 'Altérée de la Dominante' ou la gamme 'Augmentée-Diminuée'. Elle est le dernier (septième) mode de la gamme mineur mélodique (ascendante).

Nous ne savons pas exactement comment Charlie Parker voyait ces relations, c'est à dire s'il envisageait des accords avec des extensions, ou des gammes construites sur des accords, ou (plus probable) un peu des deux.

En quelques instances, il est évident que Parker pense en fonction des gammes. Par exemple, mesure 8 de son premier refrain solo dans *Au Privave* est pratiquement (à part la dernière note) une gamme harmonique descendante de Sol, jouée au-dessus de ses accords II 7 et V 7 (La∅ et Re 7).

Des notes simplement chromatiques (qu'on n'est pas obligé de 'justifier' au point de vue des accords ou des gammes) entrent aussi dans beaucoup des phrases de Parker (par exemple, le solo de *Au Privave*, premier refrain, mesure 7).

Tout compte fait, la sélection des notes que fait Parker sert à illustrer la maxime ancienne, que n'importe quelle note 'collera' avec un accord, pourvu qu'on sache comment la résoudre. Pour des étudiants de l'improvisation de jazz au-dessus des progressions d'accords, le 'comment' est la question difficile. C'est là qu'une étude détaillée du style et des pensées musicales de Parker est de grande valeur, si ce n'est indispensable.

Il faut accorder autant d'attention aux qualités rythmiques de Parker qu'à son choix des notes. Les deux aspects fonctionnent ensemble pour mettre des phrases en relief imprévu, ce qui fait perdre agréablement l'équilibre à celui qui écoute. Le swing puissant de Parker est renforcé par son usage de l'accentuation contrastée des temps forts et faibles. Celle-ci fonctionne à plusieurs niveaux: du temps même, des demi-temps, et des quart-temps. Un effet particulier de quelques-unes des phrases est de disloquer le rythme harmonique en faisant croire qu'un nouvel accord tombe juste avant ou après là où on l'attendait (voir le solo de *Ornithology*, dernier refrain, mesures 31-2).

À part la teneur détaillée, et harmonique et rythmique, des phrases de Parker, c'est la construction des solos d'un bout à l'autre qui exige de l'admiration. Sur ce point, le critique français, André Hodeir fait une observation révélatrice: "Il semble sans doute que Parker fût le premier à réussir le coup difficile d'introduire dans le jazz une certaine discontinuité mélodique qui échappe, pourtant, à l'incohérence." *

En conclusion on peut dire que le grand talent de Parker réside dans la production d'une ligne mélodique toujours nouvelle et variée qui possède, bien qu'elle soit improvisée, la qualité d'une composition finie detaillée - et qui devrait exciter l'envie de presque n'importe quel compositeur.

Les Transcriptions et Comment les Utiliser

En suivant la propre méthode de Parker quand il étudiait Lester Young, son influence majeure, ces transcriptions ont été préparées en ralentissant les enregistrements à moitié de vitesse (à l'octave au-dessous du ton original) afin de pouvoir vérifier exactement chaque note. (Peter Burden, un saxophoniste admirable qui a de l'oreille pour Parker, a eu la gentillesse de vérifier quelques-unes des phrases les plus difficiles à double-temps).

Bien sûr, vous pouvez jouer les thèmes et les solos comme s'ils étaient n'importe quelle autre composition notée. Mais ceci n'est pas le but principal de l'utilisation des transcriptions de jazz, qui est d'apprendre à improviser en suivant des exemples. Mémorisez les thèmes et les séquences d'accords, mais pas forcement les solos en entier. Choisissez certaines phrases, analysez-les par rapport aux accords qui les accompagnent, et mémorisez-les. Référez-vous à la section 'Phrases Choisies', où on a rassemblé et classifié des phrases typiques de Parker. Des phrases sur les progressions II-V et II-V-I peuvent être travaillées dans toutes les tonalités. Cela vous servira comme préparation pour improviser sur ces progressions quand elles se présenteront dans d'autres airs et d'autres tonalités. C'est tout à fait correct d'inclure quelques phrases note pour note de Parker dans vos propres improvisations, si le contexte (les accords) le permet. Développez vos propres variantes en partant de ces emprunts.

Il est essentiel d'écouter les enregistrements originaux. La plupart se font constamment copiés parmi des émissions et des compilations diverses, et en cherchant un peu dans les magasins de disques et les bibliothèques on devrait arriver à les trouver. En cas de difficulté on peut s'adresser à un magasin spécialiste de jazz, tels que Ray's Jazz Shop ou Mole Jazz (Londres).

* d'après Robert George Reisner, *Bird*: The Legend of Charlie Parker (Citadel Press 1962)

L'Accompagnement

Les séquences d'accords pour la plupart des airs de jazz, y compris le répertoire de Parker, sont composées de cinq ou six types fondamentaux d'accords. Les voici:

TYPE	DISTRIBUTION CONVENTIONELLE DES NOTES DANS L'ACCORD	SYMBOLE
7me majeure		C△
7me de dominante		C7
7me mineure		Cm7
7me mi-diminuée		C⏀
7me mineure/majeure		Cm△
7me diminuée		Co

Pour l'accompagnement, la distribution la plus simple des notes de ces accords (au piano ou à la guitare) est d'inclure seulement la fondamentale, 3^{ce} et 7me et de négliger la 5te. Au piano, la fondamentale devrait être prise par la main gauche, et la 3^{ce} et 7me par la main droite. En distribuant les notes ainsi, la 7me mineure sert aussi comme la 7me mi-diminuée, ce qui réduit la liste des accords à cinq types différents.

Ce procédé est connu comme la distribution du 'moins de notes' dans l'accord. En y ajoutant l'idée de mener les voix par 'le moins de mouvement', on peut jouer une séquence de II-V-I ainsi:

| Dm7 | G7 | C△ | Dm7 | G7 | C△ |

Cette combinaison de l'accord et la façon de mener les voix peut être résumée comme le principe du 'moins de notes et le moins de mouvement'. Il peut s'appliquer à la plupart des séquences d'accords

dans le jazz, y compris celles de cette collection.

Les 1ers ou 2mes renversements sont parfois nécessaires pour satisfaire la ligne de basse. On les indique en écrivant le symbole de l'accord au-dessus de la note de basse appropriée:

$$\frac{F7}{A} \qquad \frac{F7}{C}$$

1er renversement   2me renversement

La disposition des accords dans les parties de piano notées est basée sur le principe du 'moins de notes et le moins de mouvement', mais parfois avec l'addition d'une ou encore plus d'extensions (9me, 11me, 13me) aussi bien que des 5tes augmentées ou diminuées où il le faut. Les accompagnements se rapprochent de ceux des pianistes préférés de Parker - Duke Jordan, Al Haig - aux enregistrements originaux, mais il ne s'agit pas de transcriptions exactes. Ross Russell fait une bonne description du style de Haig qui consiste à accompagner avec des accords ('comping'): 'Haig ne joue pas du piano à temps égal, ou à quatre temps reguliers... Ses accords sont bien choisis, disposés et nuancés, et ils cadrent bien avec la structure du rythme dont il fait partie.'[*]

Les intervalles d'un accord devant être élevés sont précédés du signe +. (Tout seul, le + indique

---

* Ross Russell, *Bird Lives* (Quartet Books 1973)

une 5te augmentée). Les intervalles devant être abaissés sont précédés du signe ♭. Un symbole de la dominante suivi par 'sus 4' indique que la 3^{ce} est remplacée par une 4te.

Les accords notés pour piano sont écrits à 'temps égal', c'est à dire comme des blanches qui tombent sur le temps, mais bien sûr l'accompagnateur doit varier le placement rythmique des accords afin d'arriver à un style authentique du 'comping' (comme évoqué par la description précédente du style de Haig).

Les parties pour piano sont destinées à accompagner les thèmes, mais normalement elles iront aussi très bien avec les solos. Il y a parfois (dans *Ornithology*, par exemple) des différences légères entre la séquence d'accords jouée pour le thème et la séquence jouée pour l'improvisation.

Les pianistes qui désirent exécuter ces transcriptions seront obligés de jouer un accompagnement en accords de la main gauche. En effet, une ligne de basse composée des notes singulières prises du fond des accords écrits suffira très bien. Au-dessus de celle-ci, on peut ajouter la 3^{ce} et la 7me (ou bien la 7me et la 3^{ce}) pour remplir l'harmonie de base. Ceux qui n'arriveraient pas à tendre assez la main gauche pour jouer la fondamentale, la 7me et la 3^{ce} (c'est à dire d'embrasser une 10me), peuvent se passer de la fondamentale ou de la 3^{ce} (10me).*

Discographie des Transcriptions

Les dates et les personnels des enregistrements en ordre chronologique.

Moose the Mooche, Hollywood, le 28 mars 1946
Parker (saxophone alto), Miles Davis (trompette), Lucky Thompson (saxophone ténor), Dodo Marmarosa (piano), Arvin Garrison (guitare), Vic McMillan (contrebasse), Roy Porter (batterie)
À trouver sur *'Bird' Symbols*, Charlie Parker Records PLP-407 et *Charlie Parker on Dial* Vol.1, Spotlite Records 101

Scrapple from the Apple, New York, le 4 novembre 1947
Parker, Davis, Duke Jordan (piano), Tommy Potter (contrebasse), Max Roach (batterie)
À trouver sur *Memorial Charlie Parker*, Vogue CLD.753 (une autre version se trouve sur l'album *'Bird' Symbols*)

Au Privave, New York, le 17 janvier 1951
Parker, Davis, Walter Bishop (piano), Teddy Kotick (contrebasse), Max Roach (batterie)
À trouver sur *Swedish Schnapps (The Genius of Charlie Parker #8)*, Verve V6-8010

Blues for Alice, New York, le 8 août 1951
Parker, Red Rodney (trompette), John Lewis (piano), Ray Brown (contrebasse), Kenny Clarke (batterie)
À trouver aussi sur *Swedish Schnapps* (voir ci-dessus)

Confirmation, New York, le 4 août 1953
Parker, Al Haig (piano), Percy Heath (contrebasse), Max Roach (batterie)
À trouver sur *Now's the Time (The Genius of Charlie Parker #3)*, Verve/Polydor 2304095 Mono

Ornithology, Boston, le 22 septembre 1953
Parker, Red Garland (piano), Bernie Griggs (contrebasse), Roy Haynes (batterie)
À trouver sur *Charlie Parker at Storyville*, Blue Note BT 85108

*Pour plus de renseignements sur la disposition des accords, voir Lionel Grigson, *Practical Jazz* (Stainer & Bell 1988)

Commentaire sur les Thèmes et les Solos

(Les phrases appelées a), b), etc. dans le texte sont marquées ainsi dans les transcriptions.)

1. AU PRIVAVE (1951)
Forme: Blues de douze mesures

THÈME

Ce thème optimiste d'un tempo vif moyen est assez typique d'une 'tête' de blues de Parker, organisé d'une série de motifs mélodiques et rythmiques courts qui forment ensemble une phrase de douze mesures presque continue. Les mesures 1-3 font une assertion forte de la tonique au ton majeur, négligeant l'accord de la sous-dominante habituel de la 2me mesure d'un blues. Les phrases au début d'une tête de blues de Parker sont souvent ainsi, proches de l'accord parfait majeur en comprenant la note sensible, plutôt que la 7me bémolisée de la gamme du blues. La 7me bémolisée (Mi ♭) est gardée, comme au blues traditionel, jusqu'à la quatrième mesure, pour annoncer la sous-dominante qui arrive.

Dans ses thèmes de blues, les énonciations plus ouvertement 'blues' de Parker, qui utilisent les notes de la gamme blues, sont des fois réservées pour les accords de la sous-dominante des mesures 5 et 6 - comme dans *Au Privave* et dans l'autre blues de cette collection, *Blues for Alice*

Il faut remarquer la structure rythmique positive de chaque motif, et l'utilisation des syncopes pour changer certaines notes. Les mesures 1 et 2 impliquent une contre-mesure de 3+3+2 temps contre la mesure à **4/4**. La figure dans la mesure 5 a une structure pareille, mais à la croche. Celle-ci est aussi la figure rythmique principale (1re mesure etc.) de *Moose the Mooche*.

SOLO - *trois refrains (36 mesures)*
PREMIER REFRAIN

a) Cette phrase est placée sur les mesures 2 et 3 c'est à dire au milieu des quatres premières mesures plutôt qu'au début. Encore une fois, la sous-dominante est négligée à l'avantage d'une phrase clairement tonique. La mélodie du 2me temps de la 2me mesure jusqu'au 2me temps de la 3me mesure est une transposition exacte des cinqs premiers temps du thème d'*Ornithology* - mais elle commence sur un temps faible au lieu d'un temps fort. La dernière note de la phrase entière présente 1 temps ½ à l'avance la 7me bémolisée de la mesure 4. Parker se sert aussi de cette anticipation - la '7me en avance' - dans les solos de *Blues for Alice* (premier refrain, mesure 3) et *Confirmation* (premier refrain, mesure 27).

b) Deux motifs courts, chacun précédé d'une levée de quatre doubles-croches, au-dessus de la sous-dominante dans les mesures 5 et 6. Le deuxième motif est presque une reprise du premier, mais avec Re ♭, ce qui implique la sous-dominante mineure, au lieu de Re (bécarre).

c) D'une durée de presque 4 mesures ½, cette phrase est placée à travers la division entre la seconde et les quatre dernières mesures du refrain. Elie est construite d'une enchaînement de deux 'phrases d'approche' - d'abord à l'accord de la sus-tonique (Gm7, mesure 9) et puis, continuant sans pause, à la mesure 11.

La mesure 7 est l'archétype du 'bop break'; une phrase d'une croche et un triolet qui monte de la note sensible à travers l'accord parfait de la tonique, suivie par une descente chromatique de la note sensible (comparer le break au solo qui commence dans la mesure 31 du thème d'*Ornithology*).

La mesure 8 sert à illustrer une approche standard de Parker à l'accord de la sus-tonique (dans cette tonalité, Gm7) pour commencer les quatre dernières mesures d'un blues. À part la dernière note, cette mesure est pratiquement une gamme harmonique descendante de Sol mineur, jouée au-dessus des ses accords II 7 et V 7 (A ∅ et D7). Pour un exemple d'une autre façon d'approcher la sus-tonique, voir le solo de *Blues for Alice*, deuxième refrain, mesure 8.)

Enchâssé dans la mesure 9 (notes 2-5) il y a une phrase d'une croche et un triolet qui monte comme celle de mesure 7, mais transposée pour commencer sur la 9me de Gm7. Dans les mesures 10 et 11, la ligne se compose autour d'un mouvement ascendant de la 5te à la 5te augmentée de la dominante (C7) jusquà la 3^{ce} de la tonique (Fa).

DEUXIÈME REFRAIN

d) Une phrase qui réaffirme la tonique d'une manière forte et charmante, et qui souligne en même temps la mesure de **4/4** en plaçant les tons evidents de l'accord (la fondamentale et la 5te) sur les temps 1 et 3 de la mesure 1.

e) Une longue phrase serpentante de 5 mesures, qui commence d'une levée de trois croches dans la mesure 2, et qui s'approche de la mesure 5 (sous-dominante) d'un mouvement descendant, pour continuer à travers les mesures 5 et 6 au retour de la tonique dans la mesure 7. A partir de la levée jusqu'aux mesure 3 et 4 le choix des notes par rapport aux accords rompt la mesure d'une façon qui n'est pas facile à analyser. En commençant du quatrième temps de la mesure 2, les notes semblent s'arranger en trois mesures à **3/4**. La ligne se resoud sur B ♭ 7

44

(mesure 5) et continue en haut d'un motif vigoureux qui comprend la 9ᵐᵉ bémolisée (Si) la 11ᵐᵉ augmentée (Mi) et la 13ᵐᵉ (Sol), avant de revenir sans détour à la tonique.

f) Un silence de quatre temps précède la levée de quatre doubles-croches à une spécialité de Parker - le 'corkscrew' (tire-bouchon) à double-temps au-dessus de Gm7 et C7 jusqu'à F. L'effet du 'corkscrew' se trouve dans la première moitié de la mesure de Gm7 (mesure 9):

Gm7

Bienque Parker se serve souvent de cette formule, il arrive toujours à laisser celui qui écoute dans le doute sur la façon dont il va continuer. Dans ce cas-ci, il continue à double-temps pendant le reste de la mesure et la mesure suivante (C7), en utilisant un chromatisme saisissant (+5 et ♭9) dans la deuxième moitié de la mesure, avant de resoudre la phrase sur la 5ᵗᵉ de la tonique dans la mesure 11.

TROISIÈME REFRAIN

g) Parker embellit les deux dernières mesures du deuxième refrain de deux fioritures gracieuses qui mènent sans pause à une phrase de blues terre-à-terre dans les mesures 1-3 - en effet c'est la première utilisation des notes blues (la 5ᵗᵉ bémolisée et la 3ᶜᵉ bémolisée de la gamme du blues) jusqu'ici dans ce solo.

h) Une levée de trois notes dans la mesure 4, partant d'une 9ᵐᵉ anticipée de F7, conduit à une phrase qui descend à travers la sous-dominante (B♭7), et qui est, en effet, écourtée sur le dernier temps de la mesure 5. Après un silence de deux temps, un motif d'un triolet lent (qui implique la sous-dominante mineure) nous ramène à la tonique (mesure 7). Malgré le silence qui les sépare, les deux parties de cette phrase forment une seule idée complète.

i) Encore une phrase d'approche à la sus-tonique (comparer la mesure 8 à la mesure correspondante du premier refrain), avec un silence après le premier temps de la mesure 9. La phrase entière fait en sorte de donner l'impression d'être jouée avec un temps de retard - si elle commençait un temps plus tôt, elle se terminerait naturellement sur le dernier temps de la mesure 8 (avec la croche finale comme anticipation du prochain temps frappé).

j) Après un silence de 1 temps ¹/₂, une levée de trois croches conduit à la dominante (C7) dans la mesure 10, sur le premier temps duquel Parker fait sonner aussi bien la 9ᵐᵉ bémole que dièse (augmentée) dans

un doublé d'un triolet qui continue jusqu'à la mesure 11. La resolution de la phrase est retardée jusqu'au troisième temps, après avoir évoqué l'interpolation de IV mineur dans la première moitié de la mesure.

k) Une phrase simple pour dire 'au-revoir' qui mène de la fin du refrain jusqu'au prochain.

2. SCRAPPLE FROM THE APPLE (1947)
Forme: AABA 32 mesures

Un enregistrement alternatif de cette version (une des premières) pour quintette. Les changements des accords pour les sections A sont fondamentalement ceux de *Honeysuckle Rose* de Fats Waller (un air que Parker avait enregistré étant adolescent), tandis que les changements de la section B ('middle 8') sont ceux de *I Got Rhythm* (transposé en Fa).
Les progressions de *Scrapple* sont, alors, un hybride de deux séquences AABA d'accords.

THÈME

Les quatre premières mesures donnent un bon exemple sur la façon dont Parker construit des phrases au-dessus de II7 et V7 au ton majeur. Dans la première mesure il faut remarquer comment les 7ᵐᵉˢ majeures et bémolisées (Fa ♯ et Fa bécarre) sont toutes les deux employées au-dessus de II7 (Gm7), et comment la 7ᵐᵉ bémolisée se resoud (après une 3ᶜᵉ qui descend) à la 5ᵗᵉ au lieu de la 3ᶜᵉ plus habituelle de la dominante (C7) dans la mesure suivante. La mesure 3 se termine sur une 9ᵐᵉ bémolisée, anticipée mais pas resolue, de C7.

Comme la plupart des thèmes de Parker, la tête de *Scrapple* est fortement rythmique et peut être jouée comme un solo à la batterie.

La section B est improvisée. La phrase *a)* franchit deux mesures de A7 et une mesure et un temps de D7. Les 9ᵐᵉˢ bémole et dièse s'entendent sur le deuxième temps de la mesure 17. Le Do ♯ au début de la mesure 19 semble être une fausse note, mais il 'appartient' au A7 de la mesure précédente.

La phrase *b)* de la section centrale est une ascension à double-temps, breve mais triomphale, à G7, qui arrive sur un Sol aigu et le tient effectivement à partir du dernier temps de la mesure 21 jusqu'au premier temps de la mesure suivante avant de descendre à la 13ᵐᵉ et à la 9ᵐᵉ. Un silence d'un temps précède la levée d'une double-croche à la phrase *c)*, encore un exemple du 'corkscrew' à double-temps au-dessus de Gm7 et C7 (les mesures 23 et 24), avec une pause avant sa fioriture finale.

SOLO - un seul refrain (32 mesures)
A₁ (1st 8)
d), e) et *f)* Les huit premières mesures se déroulent dans une série de trois phrases d'une longueur et

d'une complexité croissantes. La troisième phrase *f)*, qui est la plus longue, est caractérisée d'un chromatisme typique de passage avant de mener au début de A$_2$ (2nd 8). On peut remarquer, dans la deuxième moitié de la mesure 8, l'utilisation indirecte de A♭ m7 qui mène en montant à travers sa 7me et sa 11me (Sol ♭ et Re ♭) à la quinte (Re) de l'accord suivant (Gm7). (Comparer au solo de *Ornithology*, premier refrain, mesure 14.)

A$_2$ (2nd 8)

g) Une phrase à double-temps de C7 qui retourne à Gm7. (Exceptionellement pour Parker, elle semble être exécutée avec un peu d'inquiétude).

h) Une approche typique de Parker de la dominante à la tonique (mesures 12-13) qui continue à évoquer les secondes quatre mesures des progressions de *I Got Rhythm* plutôt que celles plus regulières de *Scrapple* - c'est à dire il y a un mouvement à la sous-dominante dans la prochaine mesure (mesure 14) et puis un retour dans la mesure suivante. Le doublé répété dans les mesures 14 et 15 semble indiquer deux mesures à **3/4** qui commencent sur le 2me temps de la mesure 14 (une contre-mesure de 1+3+3+1 au lieu de 4+4 temps). On pourrait appeler cette fin le 'tortillement'.

B ('Middle 8')

i) Une façon classique de franchir les trois premières mesures de la section centrale de *I Got Rhythm*. Les deux premières mesures (17 et 18) ressemblent à une approche de la dominante à une tonique de Re dans la troisième mesure (19) - qui continue, pourtant, à la 7me. (Comparer cette mesure à *Blues for Alice*, premier refrain, mesure 3.) Sa fin donne à cette phrase optimiste une de pointe pathétique. Si on considère le prochain G7 comme la sous-dominante de D7, la fin de la phrase aura une signification pareille à la 7me 'en avance' dans la 3me mesure d'un blues.

j) Une phrase bien conçue de cinq mesures qui mène à la première mesure du dernier A (Last 8). L'éclat harmonique de la mesure 21 est rendue grâce à l'utilisation de la 13me et la 9me ensemble avec la 11me augmentée vive de G7.

A$_3$ (Last 8)

k), *l)* et *m)* Sans compter la mesure 25 (la fin de la phrase précédente) le refrain se termine en trois phrases d'une longueur décroissante, ce qui renverse la formule de A$_1$ (1st 8).

3. MOOSE THE MOOCHE (1946)
Forme: AABA, 32 mesures ('Changements de rythme')

THÈME
Une des premières compositions sur les accords de *I Got Rhythm* qui est, peut-être, le thème le plus strictement organisé de Parker. *Moose* n'est pas facile à mémoriser à cause des différences entre le A$_1$ (1st 8) et le A$_2$ (2nd 8), et aussi parce que le B (3rd 8) est noté au lieu d'être libre pour l'improvisation. La plupart des 'têtes rythmiques' sont presque identiques pour les sections principales de 8 mesures, et alors on n'a qu'à mémoriser 8 mesures - vu que le B est improvisé.)

Le motif primaire est la figure rythmique/mélodique de la mesure 1 - encore un exemple de la division 3+3+2 de la mesure, comme au thème de *Au Privave* (mesure 5). Cette figure rythmique apparaît dans la première et la troisième mesure de chaque section de 8 mesures, aussi bien que dans les mesures 15 et 31, huit fois en tout.

Le plan mélodique/harmonique des quatre premières mesures des sections principales se reduit simplement à I-V-I-V, et ceci est suivi par un mouvement 'à la sous-dominante et de retour' dans la mélodie et les progressions des quatre prochaines mesures. Mais les secondes quatre mesures de A$_2$ (2nd 8) ont une mélodie différente qui va 'à la sous-dominante et de retour', et aussi une fin adaptée pour conduire à la section B (3rd 8) par moyen d'une 9me anticipée sur D7.

Le B ('middle 8') fait contraster des syncopes détachées (les mesures 17, 20 et 24) avec des croches courantes (les mesures 19, 21 et 22). Remarquez l'utilisation des 9mes et des 13mes au-dessus de D7 (mesure 18) et de G7 (mesure 19), ainsi que les 9mes bémole et dièse au-dessus de F7 (mesure 24).

SOLO - un seul refrain (32 mesures)
Par contraste avec le thème très 'chargé', la plupart du solo est composée de phrases plus longues, avec plus de silences.

A$_1$ (1st 8)

a) Une phrase d'ouverture qui tourne autour de la tonique.

b) Celle-ci est une phrase typique d'un mouvement 'à la sous-dominante et de retour' (en passant par IV mineur) qui commence au même temps de la mesure que la phrase précédente, mais qui en est plus longue d'une mesure et demie.

A$_2$ (2nd 8)

c) Une phrase courte qui va de la tonique à la dominante, et qui n'occupe que les deux premières mesures.

d) Une longue phrase (de presque cinq mesures) qui se place à travers les deux sections de quatres mesures de A₂ (2nd 8). Les mesures 11 et 12 s'approchent de la tonique d'une ligne qui, dans l'ensemble, y descend. Arrivée à la tonique (mesure 13) la phrase continue pendant la mesure 14 (IV et IVm) pour retourner à la tonique dans la mesure 15.

Comparer les longueurs et les placements des phrases dans ces deux premiers 'A'. Le A₁ (1st 8) consiste d'une phrase dans chaque section de quatre mesures (la symétrie). Le A₂ (2nd 8) en fait contraste avec une phrase courte qui prend les deux premières mesures, suivie par une phrase longue qui traverse les sections de quatre mesures (l'asymétrie).

B ('Middle 8')

e) Après une ascension d'une croche et d'un triolet (5ᵗᵉ, 9ᵐᵉ, 11ᵐᵉ bécarre et 13ᵐᵉ bécarre) Parker offre au premier accord du 'middle 8' un de ses effets préférés, une descente qui part de la 13ᵐᵉ en passant par une 11ᵐᵉ augmentée à une 9ᵐᵉ et à une 7ᵐᵉ, avec la répétition de la 13ᵐᵉ et la 11ᵐᵉ augmentée dans la prochaine mesure (18). Remarquez comment l'effet de la 11ᵐᵉ augmentée est repris au prochain accord (G7, mesure 19) mais non pas par moyen d'une transposition exacte du premier motif.

f) Cette phrase s'approche de la dominante (F7) en passant par sa propre dominante (C7). Avec l'addition d'une note chromatique de passage (C♭), la gamme du début de la phrase jusqu'à l'avant-dernière note de la mesure 21 est celle de Fa mineur mélodique (forme ascendante jouée en descendant). Comparer la phrase qui se termine à la mesure 23 au solo de *Scrapple*, mesure 19; au solo de *Confrimation*, deuxième refrain, mesure 12; et au même solo, mesure 30.

A₃ (Last 8)

g) Une phrase simple et gaie qui réaffirme la tonique.

h) Comme la deuxième phrase *d)* de A₂ (2nd 8), celle-ci dépasse la ligne de raccord des sections de quatre mesures. Remarquez l'approche chromatique qui passe par Dm7 et D♭m7 dans la mesure 27 à Cm7 (la sus-tonique, mesure 28) ainsi que l'utilisation d'une gamme simple de Si♭ majeur au-dessus de Cm7 et F7 dans la mesure 28.

i) Un 'au revoir' en partant de la dernière mesure pour le prochain refrain.

4. ORNITHOLOGY (1953)

Forme: ABAC, 32 mesures

THÈME

Les progressions dérivent, avec quelques changements pour adapter à la nouvelle mélodie, de la chanson *How High the Moon*. Il est probable que l'on devrait aussi reconnaitre le trompettiste Benny Harris (un premier collègue) pour la création de l'air.

La première version de *Ornithology* a été enregistrée en 1946, pendant la même séance (pour Dial Records) qui a produit *Moose the Mooche* et le *Night in Tunisia* historique. Dans les versions qui suivirent, Parker se passait des fins de figures d'un triolet jouées par tout l'ensemble pour terminer les sections de 16 mesures de l'air original (ce qui allait bien avec un premier rang de trois cors), en faveur des fins qui convenaient mieux à un ou deux cors.

Les progressions commencent par deux mesures de la tonique (Sol) et puis modulent en descendant, d'abord à Fa, en passant par Gm7 et C7, et après, par la même formule (II7 et V7 de la nouvelle tonalité) à Mi♭. Le dessin, donc, est d'une gamme majeure qui devient mineure, ce qui se révèle alors comme le premier pas du changement à la nouvelle tonalité, en préparant sa dominante.

En conséquence, Parker façonne d'abord une phrase hardie majeure, (la 1ʳᵉ mesure jusqu'au premier temps de la mesure 2), et puis en répète le début au ton mineur, avant de révéler la vraie intention de cette phrase (comme indiquée par le Fa aigu) qui est d'annoncer le ton de Fa majeur. Cette tonalité est alors 'mineurisée' pour conduire, en passant par B♭7, à Mi♭ dans la mesure 9. (Pour s'adapter à la mélodie, cet accord devrait être E♭7, et non pas E♭△ bien que ce dernier puisse être plus commode pour l'improvisation.)

Après le Mi♭, les progressions ramènent à la tonique mineure en passant par sa II7 et V7 (A∅ et D7). Les quatre dernières mesures de la section B (2nd 8) font une 'volte-face à double-longueur' (une mesure chacun de Bm7, E7, Am7 et D7) au A₂ (3rd 8). Le A₂ est une reprise du A₁ (1st 8), et la section C (Last 8) écourte à deux mesures la 'volte-face' pour arriver à la tonique pendant les deux dernières mesures – desquelles Parker se sert pour un 'break' bien envoyé à son premier refrain solo. (Comparez la première mesure de ce 'break', mesure 31, au solo de *Au Privave*, premier refrain, mesure 7.) Remarquez l'effet de la 5ᵗᵉ augmentée sur la dominante implicite (D7) dans le deuxième mesure de ce 'break'.

SOLO - *trois refrains (96 mesures)*

Dans cet enregistrement pris en direct d'une séance à un club de Boston, Parker arrive à s'étendre à travers trois refrains en entier. On ne donne pas d'analyse phrase-par-phrase, en partie à cause de la longueur du solo, mais aussi parce qu'on a déjà assez fait la description des caractéristiques essentielles du style de Parker dans cette collection, pour rendre compréhensible ce solo magnifique sans plus de commentaire.

Voici, pourtant, quelques traits marquants:

1. Les mesures 3 et 4 du premier refrain donnent un exemple d'une interprétation d'un mouvement II-V à deux mesures, au moyen de laquelle la progression de Gm7 à C7 devient Gm Gm△|Gm7 C7, ce qui permet la construction de la phrase autour de la ligne descendante en blanches de Sol-Fa♯-Fa♮-Mi.

2. La phrase *n)* est une citation surprenante, et rythmiquement libre, de la chanson *Tenderly* (d'origine à 3/4 temps).

3. Le point culminant du solo, juste après le milieu, arrive au A_2 (3rd 8) du deuxième refrain. Il est annoncé pendant les mesures 16 et 17 (la fin du B (2nd 8)) par une roulade descendante abrupte qui part de Fa bécarre (la phrase *o)*) La phrase *p)* (mesure 18) est une feinte à double-temps au-dessus de la tonique - et puis Parker se lance sur un 'corkscrew' à double-temps follement compliqué (la phrase *q)*) qui s'étend par-dessus Gm7 et C7 à une mesure complète de F, pour terminer avec ce qui est presque une transposition de la première phrase du thème.

4. Vers la fin du solo il y a une phrase remarquable de 9 mesures *(z)* d'une continuité frappante, qui developpe d'abord ce qui semble être une citation, et qui mène après à une autre allusion transposée au début du thème à la mesure 25 (E♭).

5. BLUES FOR ALICE (1951)

Forme: blues de 12 mesures ('Round the Clock')

THÈME

Parker a enregistré le blues direct de *Au Privave* pour le nouvel an de 1951 (le 17 janvier). Le *Blues for Alice* contrasté a été enregistré huit mois plus tard, et il est organisé autour de la variante des progressions de blues appelée diversement 'Bird Blues' ou 'Swedish Blues' ou (en Angleterre) 'Round the Clock' blues.

Voici la façon la plus simple de representer les progressions de *Alice*, par rapport à celles de base du blues modern:

PROGRESSIONS DE BASE

F		B♭7		F		F7	
B♭7		B♭7		F		D7	
Gm7		C7		F	D7	Gm7	C7	

ALICE

F		A7		Dm		F7	
B♭		B♭m		F		A♭o	
Gm7		C7		F	D7	Gm7	C7	

Les différences principales se trouvent dans les huit premières mesures. Pendant les quatre premières, les progressions de *Alice* mènent au ton du mineur relatif dans la 3me mesure. Au cours des quatre suivantes, le retour à la tonique passe par IVm, et l'approche à la sus-tonique est l'accord diminué au-dessus de III.

Dans une forme plus schématisée (la séquence stricte de 'Round the Clock') les progressions de *Alice* deviendraient:

F△	Em7 / E∅	A7	Dm7	G7	Cm7	F7	
B♭△	B♭m7	E♭7	Am7	D7	A♭m7	D♭7	
Gm7	C7		F△	D7	Gm7	C7	||

Bien que la formule 'Round the Clock' fournisse un accompagnement au thème et au solo, ceux-ci peuvent être aussi bien accompagnés par les progressions plus simples données ci-dessus (John Lewis, au piano, est plus proche de celles-ci à certains moments). Pour le dire autrement, Parker ne compte pas sur les accords de passage, et peut reduire une séquence à ses progressions essentielles.

La modulation la plus difficile qu'on trouve dans les progressions de *Alice* est celle qui est impliquée (mais non pas réalisée) dans la mesure 8, par A♭m7 - D♭7 (ou bien l'un des deux tout seul): à Sol♭ majeur. Remarquez la mélodie à ce point du thème, et en plus la phrase au même point du deuxième refrain du solo - toutes les deux sont des variantes de la première phrase de *Honeysuckle Rose*, transposée au demi-ton superieur.

Pour la plupart, le thème court à travers les progressions, et n'est pas comme un blues; les quatre dernières notes de la mesure 4, pourtant, et la mesure 5 en entier font une phrase de blues qui vient du fond du coeur (comparer à la mesure 5 de *Au Privave*).

SOLO - *Trois refrains (36 mesures)*

PREMIER REFRAIN

a) La mesure 1 s'appuye sur la 7me majeure de la tonique sur les temps 1 et 3 (de la dissonance sur les temps forts), et la mesure 2 semble se diriger vers le mineur relatif d'une manière assez simple. Mais dans la mesure 3, Parker évite la résolution attendue pour anticiper, à sa place, les accords de la prochaine mesure - encore un exemple de la '7me en avance'.

b) Une phrase de blues qui vient du fond du coeur par-dessus de IV et IVm (les mesures 5 et 6) qui ramène à la tonique (ou à III7) dans la mesure 7. Les trois dernières notes de cette mesure sont identiques à celles de la mesure 3, mais cette fois avec une autre signification - le Mi♭ anticipe les accords de la mesure 8.

c) Une phrase courte au-dessus de la sus-tonique.

d) Une autre variante du 'corkscrew' à double-temps, qui commence cette fois au-dessus de V7 plutôt que II7.

DEUXIÈME REFRAIN

e) Une variante ou un développement de la première phrase *a)* du premier refrain, qui s'étend maintenant à la mesure 4. Les mesures 3 et 4 sont prises par deux motifs dont chacun commence par un doublé, semblant d'abord indiquer Re mineur, puis subtilement varié pour évoquer F7, et placés pour diviser les deux mesures en 3+3+2 temps.

f) Comme dans le refrain précédent, cette phrase commence comme une phrase de blues au-dessus de IV et IVm, et s'étend pour terminer par une transposition ingénieuse d'une idée familière pour s'adapter aux accords de la mesure 8.

g) A double-temps au-dessus de II-V-I. Cette phrase semble commencer exprès par un faux départ - comme si Parker voulait que celui qui écoute s'attende encore à un 'corkscrew', mais elle s'interrompt pour continuer d'une façon différente.

TROISIÈME REFRAIN

h) Une note tenue expressivement après la dernière mesure du refrain précédent conduit à une figure brève de tonique dans la mesure 1.

i) Cette phrase va au mineur relatif et après à la 7ᵐᵉ de tonique. Comparez la mesure 2 aux mesures correspondantes des deux premiers refrains - chacune est composée des mêmes éléments (au fond, une gamme de Re mineur mélodique), mais chaque fois ils sont manoeuvrés d'une manière différente.

j) et *k)* sont marquées commes des phrases indépendantes, vu qu'un silence de 1 temps ¹/₂ les sépares, mais prises ensemble, elles représentent un traitement de IV et IVm dans la gamme de blues comme aux deux premiers refrains.

l) II-V-I à double-temps, comme au deuxième refrain, encore une fois caractérisé par un 'faux départ' voulu (mais avec d'autres notes).

m) Une note tenue jusqu'à la dernière mesure qui mène à un 'au-revoir' à double-temps avant le prochain refrain.

RÉSUMÉ

Dans l'ensemble, celle-ci semble être une des improvisations de blues les plus soigneusement composées de Parker. Chaque refrain est formé d'épisodes de quatre mesures: les quatre premières mesures délinéent clairement la progression au mineur relatif; les quatre secondes mesures sont caractérisées par une phrase de blues au-dessus de la sous-dominante; et les quatre dernières mesures par un retour à double-temps à la tonique. Cette similitude épisodique donne au solo complet un sens d'unité d'un bout à l'autre qui est, pourtant, équilibré, par une richesse de variation de détail entre les épisodes correspondants de chaque refrain.

6. CONFIRMATION (1953)
Forme: AABA, 32 mesures

THÈME

Les progressions harmoniques des quatre premières mesures des chaque section principale sont identiques aux quatre premières de *Blues for Alice*, c'est à dire au fond F-A7-Dm7-F7, et il est intéressant, donc, de mettre en comparaison les deux thèmes ainsi que les improvisations de Parker pendant ces sections-ci. Les progressions de *Confirmation* continuent comme un blues réduit avec une mesure de la sous-dominante, et puis se dirigent vers une demie-cadence dans le A₁ (1st 8), et vers des cadences parfaites dans le A₂ (2nd 8) et A₃ (Last 8). La section B (Middle 8) embrasse deux modulations, d'abord à la sous-dominante (Si♭) et puis à la sus-dominante bémolisée (= la médiante bémolisée de la sous-dominante); l'approche à chaque nouvelle tonalité s'effectue par une progression de II-V, et la mesure 8 est une progression de II-V qui retourne à Fa.

Contre les progressions semblables des sections principales (le A₁ (1st 8) et le A₃ (Last 8) sont identiques, et le A₂ (2nd 8) ne se distingue qu'aux deux dernières mesures), Parker a créé un thème dont les éléments sont renouvelés sans cesse. Les seules mesures identiques des sections principales sont les mesures 2 et 26, ainsi que 4-5 et 28-9. Ceci est loin d'une tête simple AABA comme *Scrapple from the Apple* lequel n'est composé uniquement que de huit mesures de musique. Néanmoins, Parker donne de l'unité au thème en créant des mesures partiellement semblables (comparez les derniers temps des mesures 1 et 25) et des mesures qui sont presque des renversements l'une de l'autre (comparez les mesures 5 et 13). Le trait le plus évident d'unification se trouve dans la manière dont les premières phrases de chaque section principale (bien qu'elles commencent différemment) se terminent par les trois mêmes syncopes.

Les deux premières mesures du B (Middle 8) se basent sur l'idée de diviser une mesure chacune de Cm7 et F7 en mi-mesures de Cm-Cm△-Cm7-F7 pour convenir à la ligne descendante de Do-Si-Si♭-La en blanches. La mélodie suit ce contour, mais elle bémolise le La attendu au 3ᵐᵉ temps de la mesure 18 jusqu'à La♭ - la 9ᵐᵉ augmentée au lieu de la 3ᶜᵉ de F7. (Comparez le solo de *Ornithology*, premier refrain, mesures 3-4.)

Remarquez la complexité de la ligne 'dégringolante' de mesure 21 (E♭ m7). La mesure 23 (D♭ △) est la dernière phrase de l'air *Woody 'n' You* par Dizzy Gillespie, jouée à double-temps.

SOLO - *Deux refrains (64 mesures)*
On ne donne pas d'analyse, pour les mêmes raisons de ne pas en avoir donné une du solo de *Ornithology*. Ces deux solos sont des chefs d'oeuvres, qui nous montrent Parker au sommet de ses capacités à l'automne de sa vie.

Translated by Peter Owens, 1989

Phrases Choisies
A. PHRASES À DOUBLE-TEMPS

1. 'CORKSCREWS' (DES TIRE-BOUCHONS)

i) *Scrapple* (1947), section centrale, phrase *c*), mesures 23 et 24

ii) *Au Privave* (1951), deuxième refrain, phrase *f*), mesures 9-11

iii) *Blues for Alice* (1951), premier refrain, phrase *d*), mesures 10 et 11

iv) *Ornithology* (1953), deuxième refrain, A₂, phrase *q*), mesures 19-22

2. D'AUTRES PHRASES À DOUBLE-TEMPS

i) *Scrapple* premier refrain, section B, phrase *b*), mesures 21 et 22

Solo, A₂, phrase *g*, mesures 10 et 11

ii)   *Blues for Alice* deuxième refrain, phrase *g*), mesures 9-11 (le 'faux départ')

Troisième refrain, phrases *l) et m*), mesures 9-11

iii) *Ornithology*, premier refrain, A_2, phrase *g*), mesures 20-22

iv)   *Confirmation*, premier refrain, A_2, phrase *d*), mesures 10-12

B.   EXTENSION ET ALTÉRATION DE LA DOMINANTE

i)   5te augmentée ascendante

Au Privave, premier refrain

ii) 5te augmentée descendante

Au Privave, deuxième refrain

iii) 9me bémole et 9me dièse

Au Privave, troisième refrain

iv) 11me augmentée (avec 13me et 9me)

Scrapple, la section B

Moose the Mooche, la section B

v)   Dominante 'altérée' (+9, ♭9, +5)

Ornithology, deuxième refrain

51

C. PHRASES DE BLUES

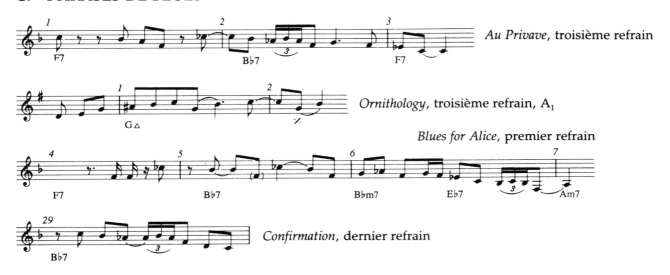

Au Privave, troisième refrain

Ornithology, troisième refrain, A$_1$

Blues for Alice, premier refrain

Confirmation, dernier refrain

D. PASSAGES DE GAMMES

Le mineur harmonique (Gm)

Au Privave, premier refrain

Majeur (Bb)

Moose the Mooche, A$_3$

Majeur (F)

Ornithology, thème, mesure 3

'Majeur harmonique' (F)

Blues for Alice, deuxième refrain, mesure 10

E. ARPÈGE

Moose the Mooche, la section B, mesure 17

Ornithology, premier refrain

52

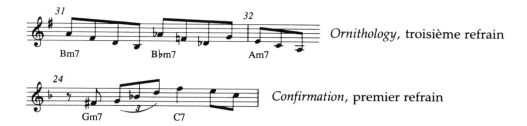

Ornithology, troisième refrain

Confirmation, premier refrain

F.   TRAITS DE RYTHME/DE MESURE
1.   DES SYNCOPES

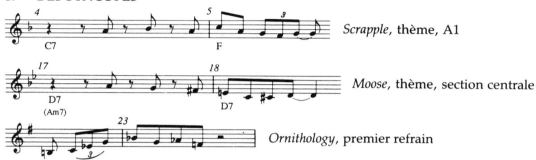

Scrapple, thème, A1

Moose, thème, section centrale

Ornithology, premier refrain

2.   LA CONTRE-MESURE

Au Privave, thème

1. AU PRIVAVE

Piano chords

(♩ = 200)

CHARLIE PARKER

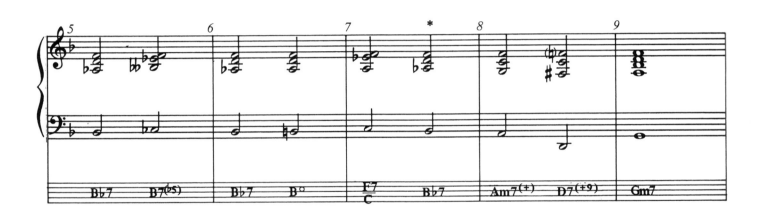

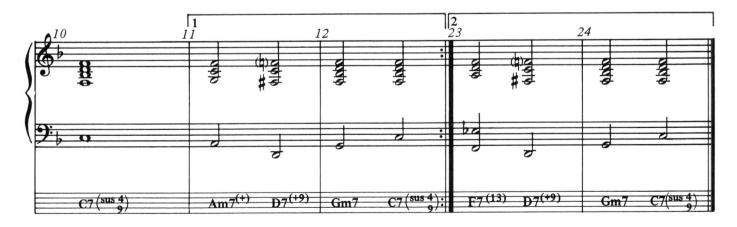

* Optional passing chord

54

1. AU PRIVAVE

Theme

CHARLIE PARKER

Solo: 1st Chorus

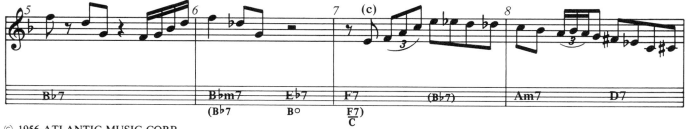

2nd Chorus

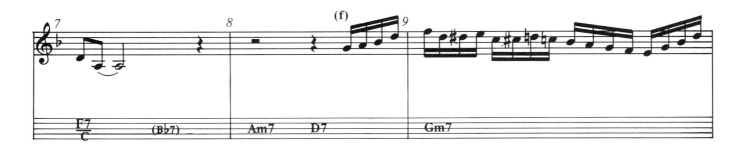

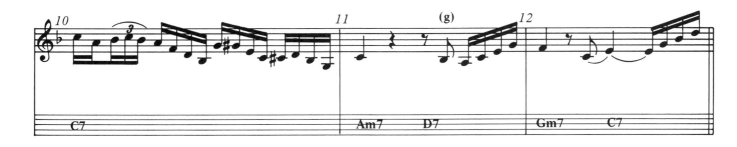

3rd Chorus

4th Chorus *(trumpet solo)*

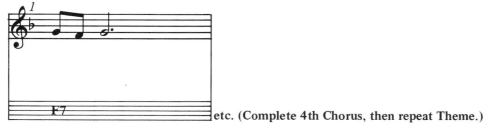

etc. (Complete 4th Chorus, then repeat Theme.)

2. SCRAPPLE FROM THE APPLE

Piano Chords

(♩ = 200)

CHARLIE PARKER

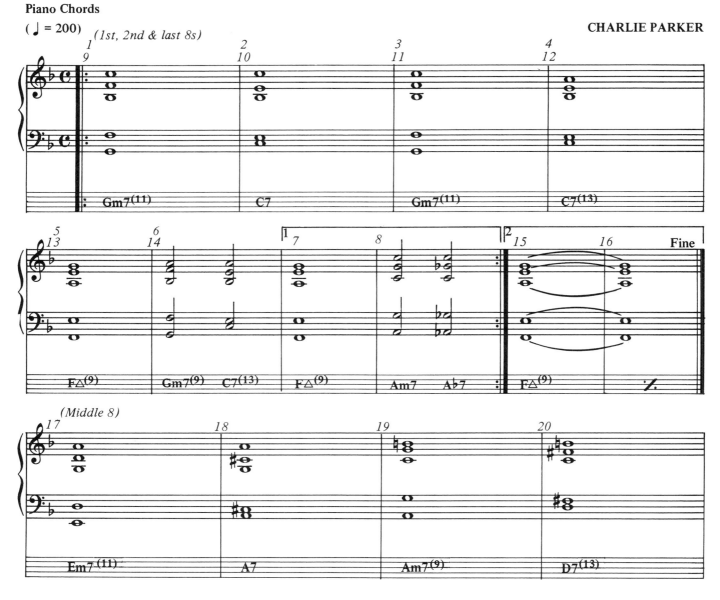

2. SCRAPPLE FROM THE APPLE

Theme

CHARLIE PARKER

(♩ = 200)

(1st & 2nd 8s)

(Middle 8 - Improvised)

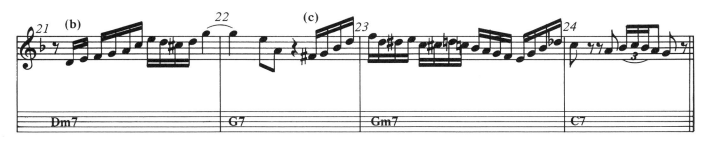

(Last 8)

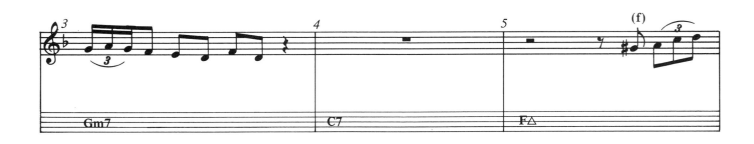

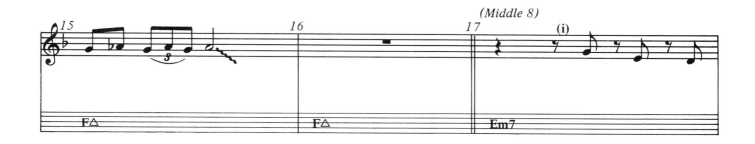

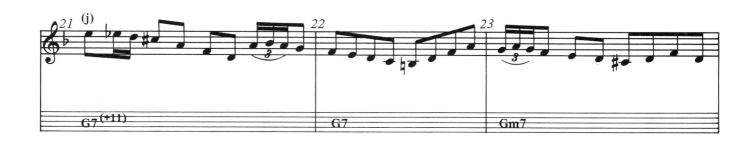

2nd Chorus *(for student)**
(1st 8)

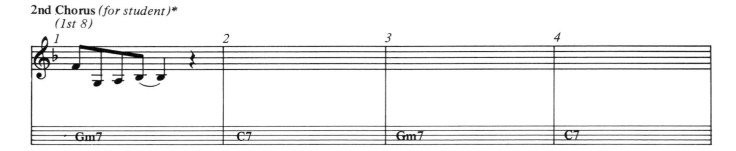

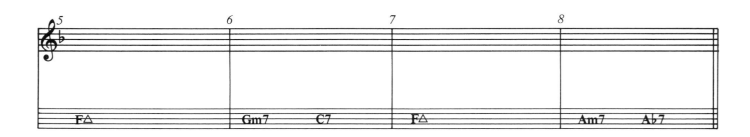

(2nd 8)

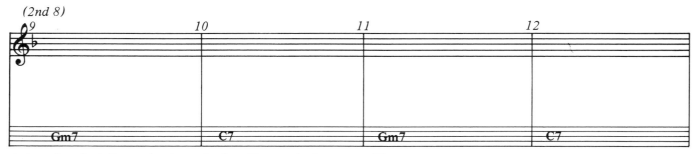

* *Complete 2nd Chorus (and any further Choruses), then repeat Theme.*

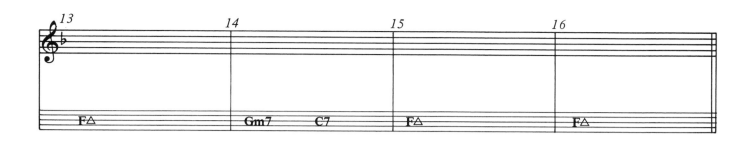

(Middle 8)

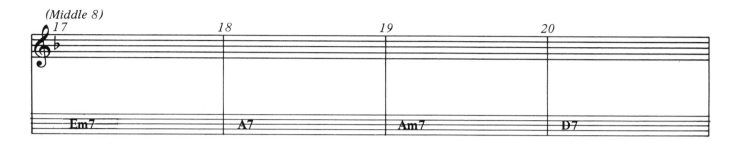

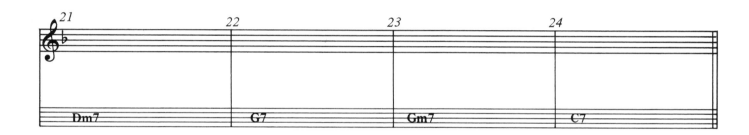

(Last 8)

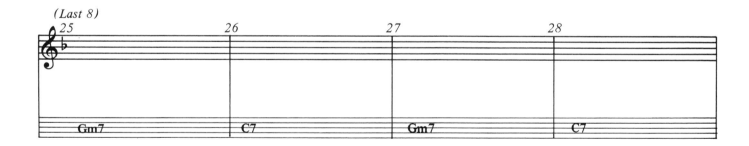

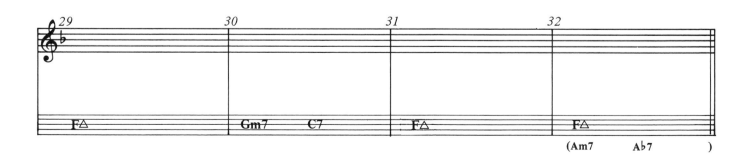

63

3. MOOSE THE MOOCHE

Piano Chords

(♩ = 224)

(1st 8)

CHARLIE PARKER

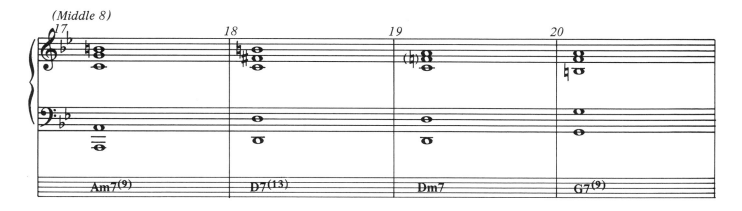

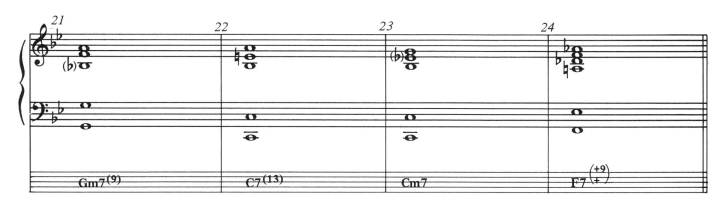

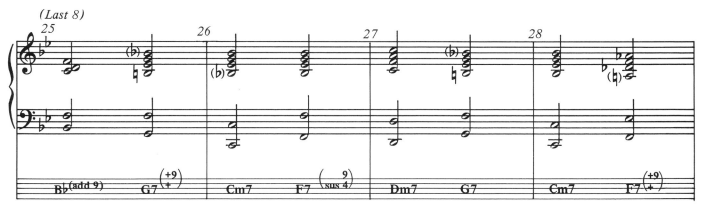

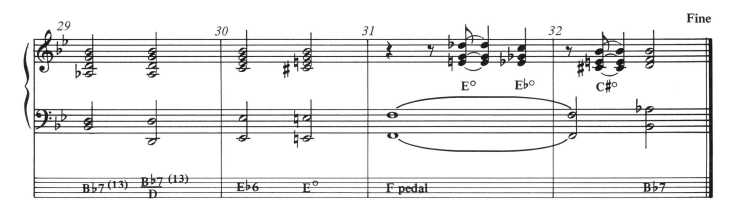

3. MOOSE THE MOOCHE

CHARLIE PARKER

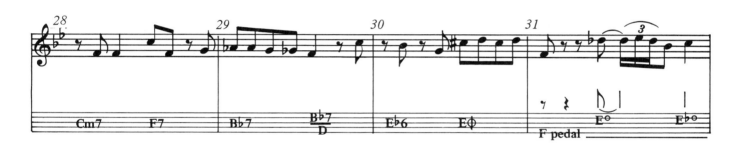

Solo 1st Chorus

Fine

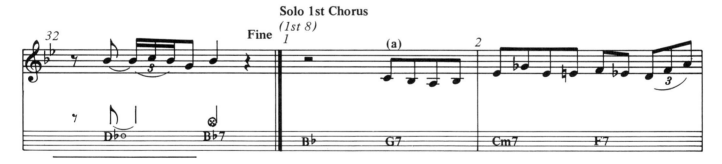

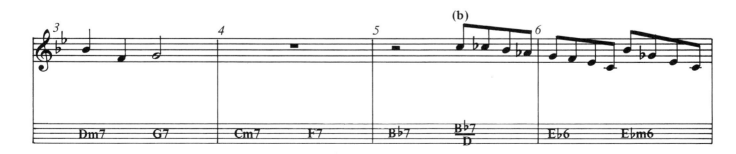

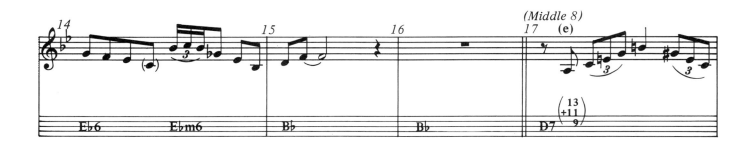

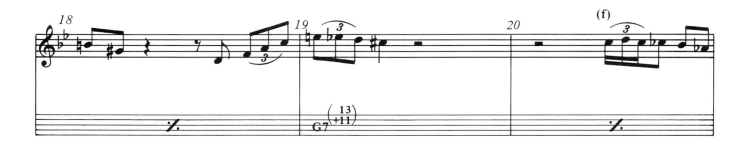

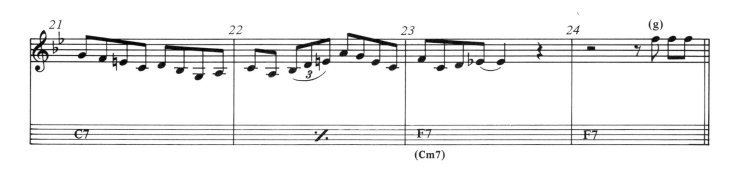

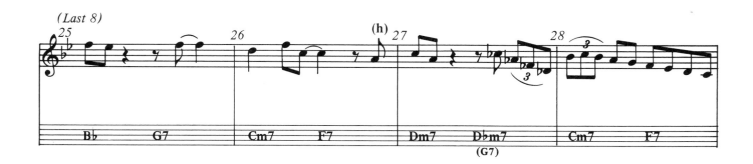

(Last 8)

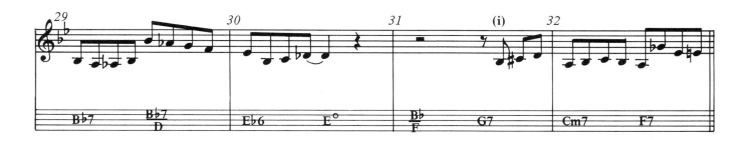

Solo: 2nd Chorus *(for student)**

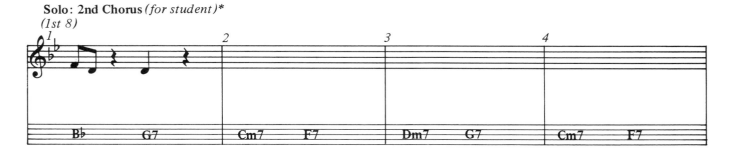

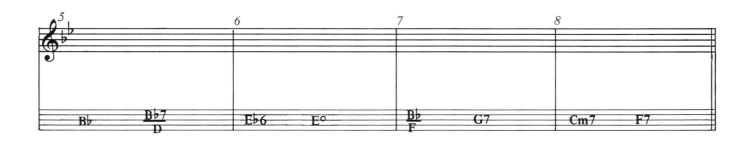

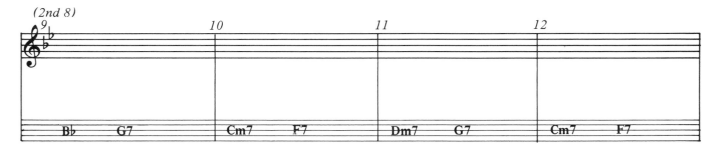

* *Complete 2nd Chorus (and any further Choruses), then repeat Theme.*

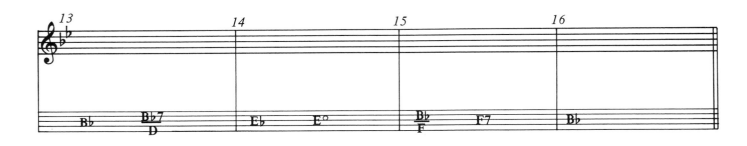

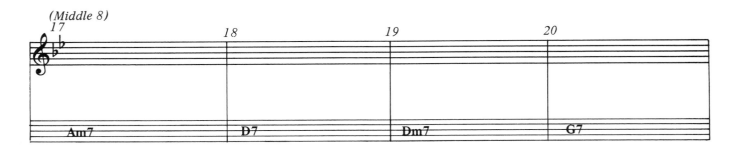

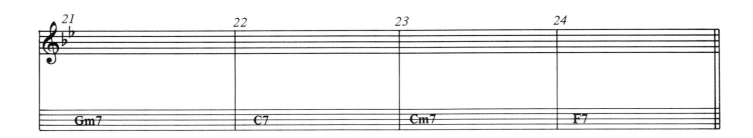

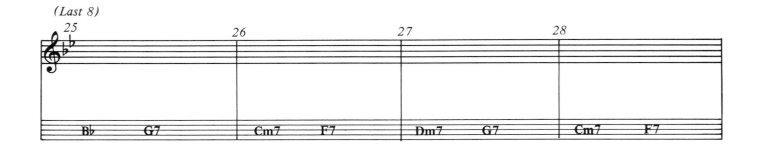

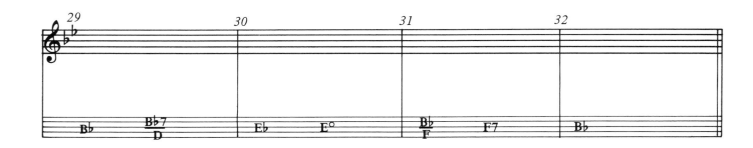

4. ORNITHOLOGY

CHARLIE PARKER
and BENNIE HARRIS

4. ORNITHOLOGY

Solo: 1st Chorus

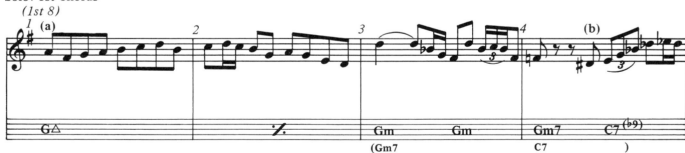

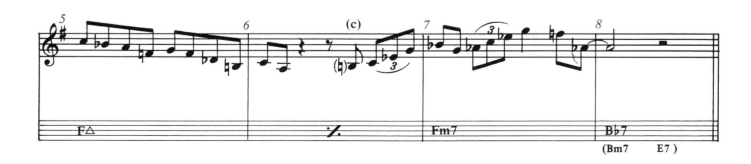

(2nd 8)

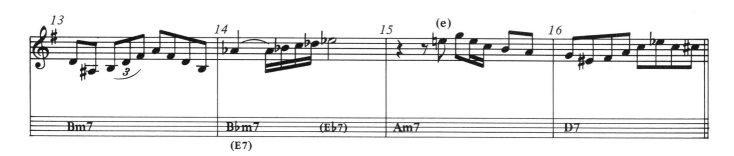

(3rd 8)

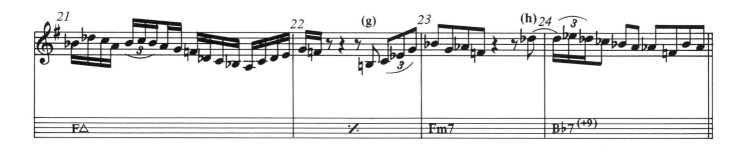

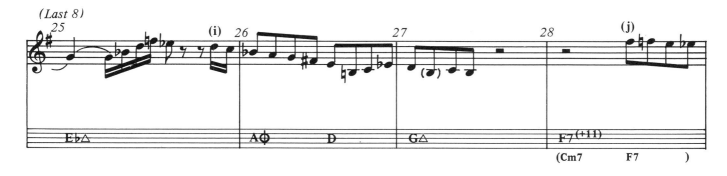

(Last 8)

2nd Chorus

(1st 8)

(2nd 8)

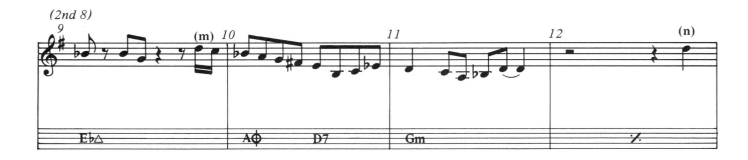

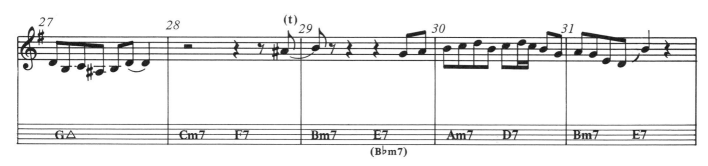

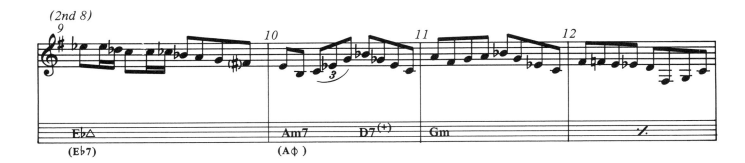

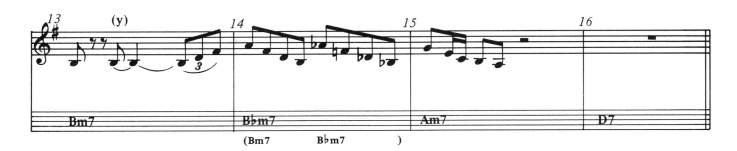

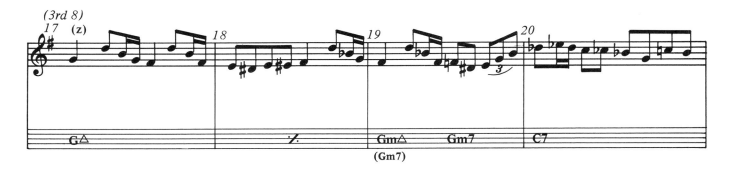

(Last 8)

4th Chorus *(for student)**

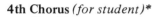

(1st 8)

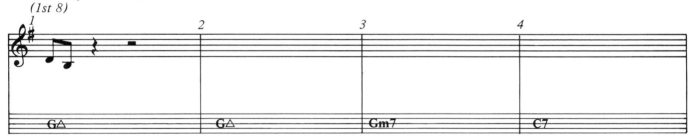

(2nd 8)

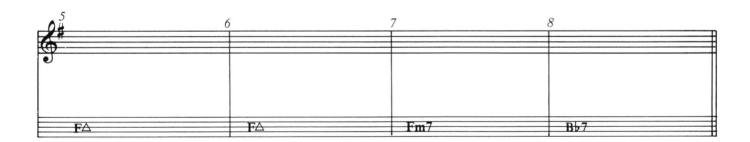

* *Complete 4th Chorus, then repeat Theme.*

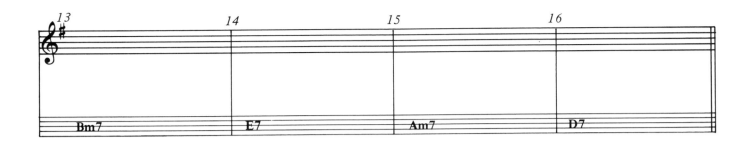

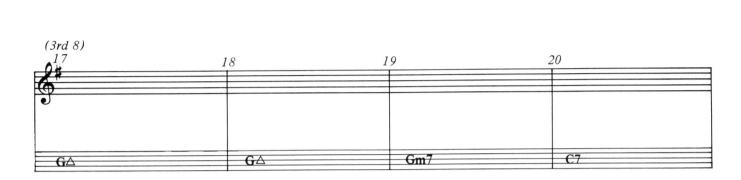

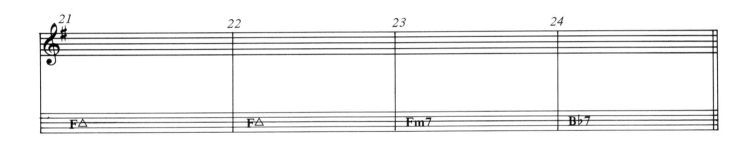

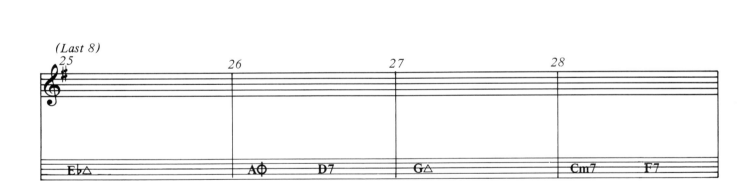

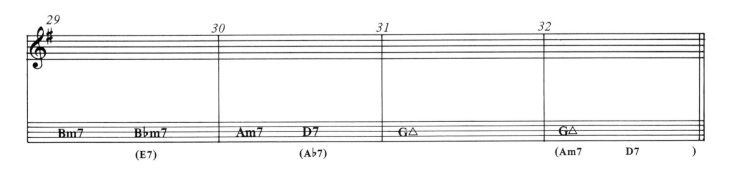

5. BLUES FOR ALICE

Piano Chords

(♩ = 165)

CHARLIE PARKER

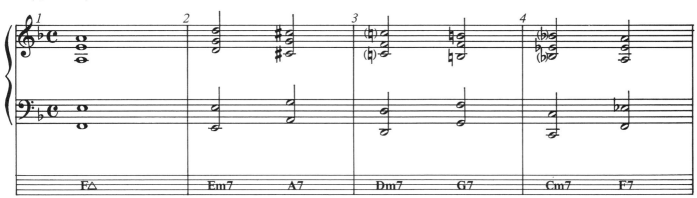

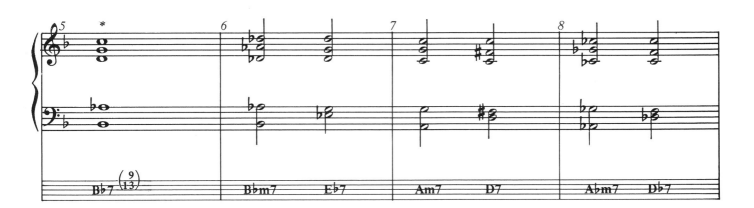

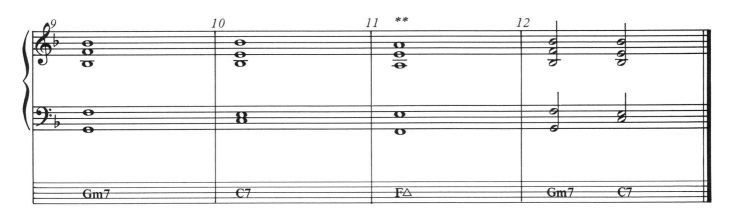

* could be **Bb△** *for solos*

** *or* **Am7   D7**

5. BLUES FOR ALICE

Theme

CHARLIE PARKER

2nd Chorus

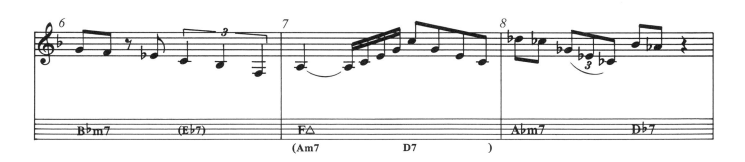

3rd Chorus

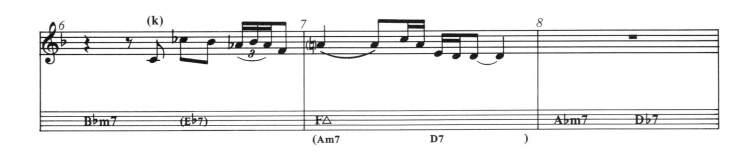

4th Chorus

etc. (Complete 4th Chorus, then repeat Theme.)

6. CONFIRMATION

Piano Chords
(♩ = 208)

CHARLIE PARKER

* bar 10: for solos play E⌀ A7

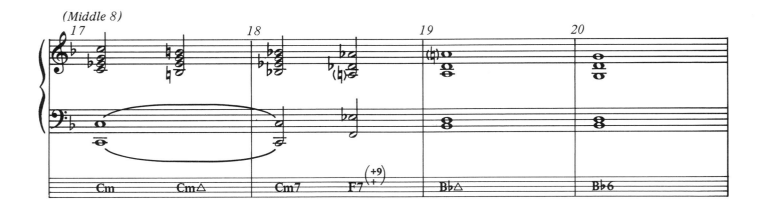

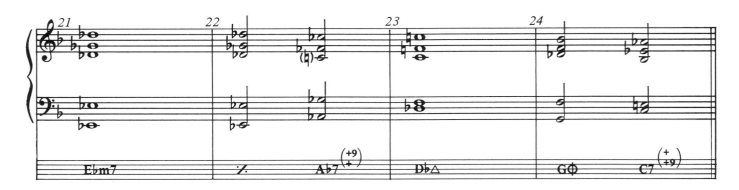

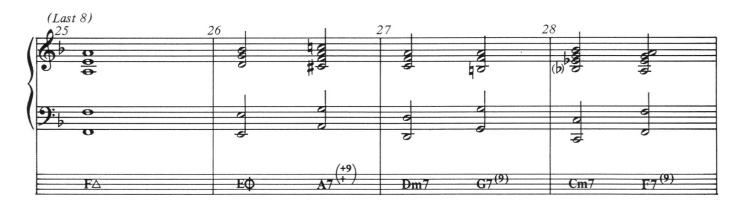

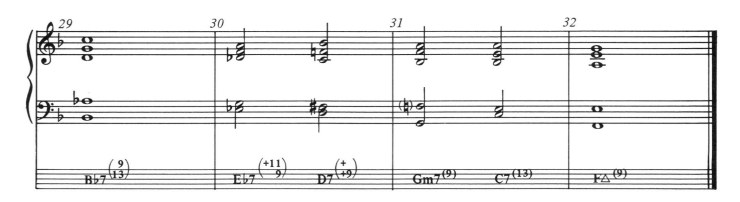

6. CONFIRMATION

Theme
(♩ = 208)

CHARLIE PARKER

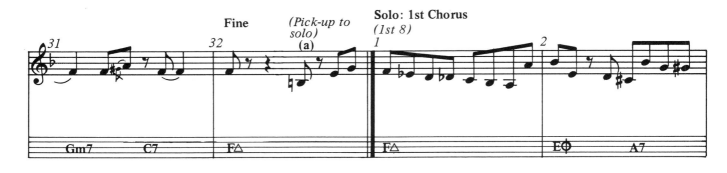

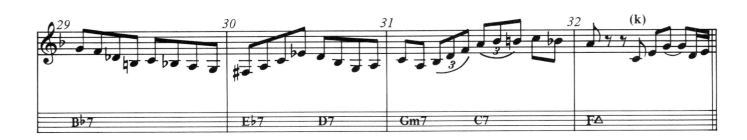

2nd Chorus

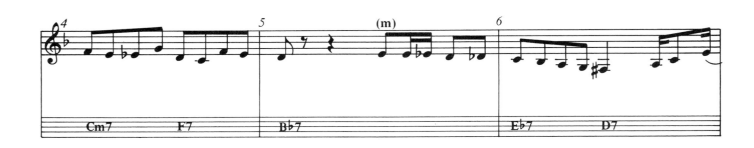

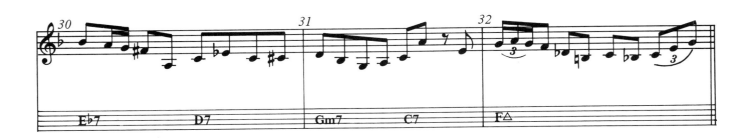

3rd Chorus *(for student)* *

(1st 8)

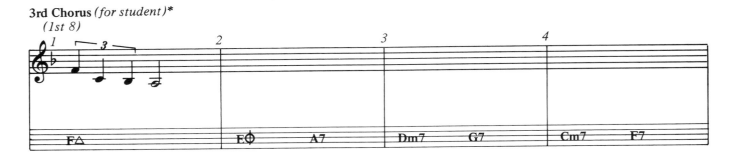

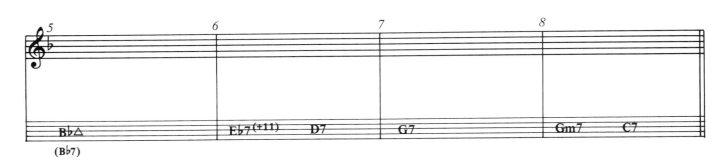

(2nd 8)

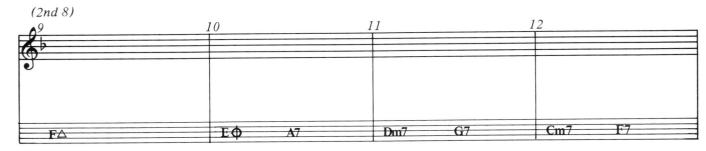

* Complete 3rd Chorus, then repeat Theme.

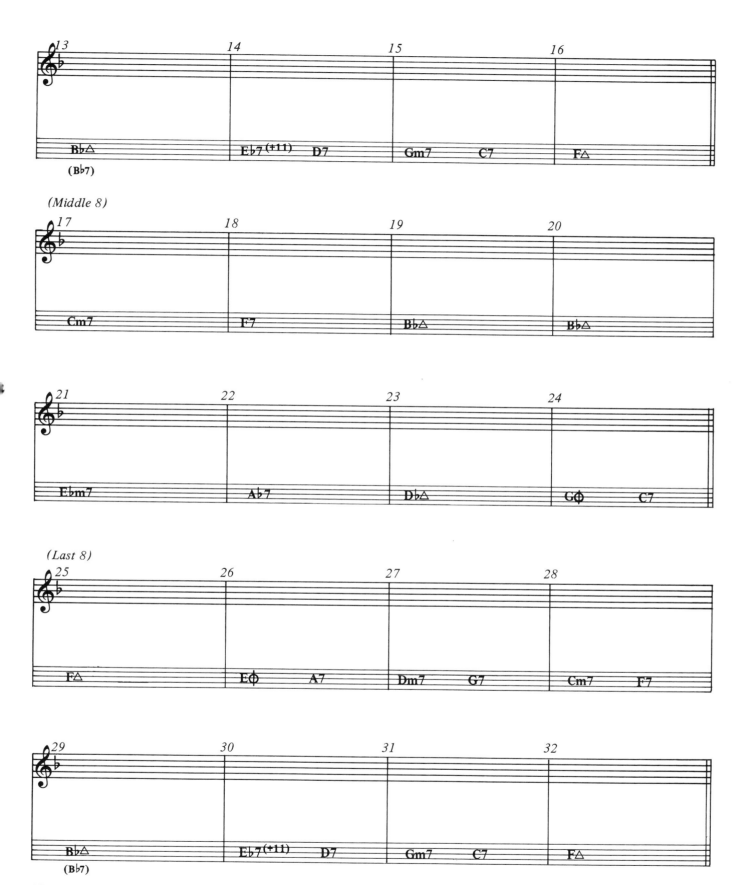

Music processed by MSS Studios, 'Rhiwlas', Dolgellau, Gwynedd. LL40 2YS
Published by Novello & Company Limited
Printed in Great Britain by The Novelle Press Limited, Sevenoaks, Kent